I0126944

Certificate

Wired2Succeed Power Charged Course

To reward you for taking the first step towards overcoming your fear barriers by purchasing *Dump Your Fear!*, Jacinth Tracey and Wired2Succeed is pleased to offer you and one guest an exclusive scholarship to attend the LIVE *Power Charged Intensive* 2-day Seminar. At this popular program, you can transform your Mind, Brain, Body and Spirit and change your life from fearFULL to powerFULL. You can forever transform your thoughts, feelings and actions and finally get the outcomes you want for your life!

To download your scholarship voucher and register, visit www.wired2succeed.com/PowerChargedLIVE.*

Use Reference # _____ when you register.

(If you were not given a reference #, use your book receipt # or promotion code)

Wired2Succeed

* This offer is open to all purchasers of *Dump Your Fear!* by Jacinth Tracey. Limit one scholarship per copy *of Dump Your Fear!* by Jacinth Tracey. Scholarship may only be applied to the *Power Charged LIVE Intensive* 2-day Seminar, and seminar registration is subject to availability and/or changes to program schedule. Please note that this is a strictly limited time offer and the scholarship must be redeemed by the date shown on the www.wired2succeed.com/PowerChargedLIVE website. The value of this scholarship is up to $3,000 as of January 2014. Additional fees and/or tuitions may apply at the time of registration. Registrants assume responsibility for all travel, food and accommodation if required and are under no additional financial obligation whatsoever to Wired2Succeed or Jacinth Tracey. Wired2Succeed and Jacinth Tracey reserve the right to refuse admission and to remove from the premises anyone whom is believed to be a disruption before, during, or after the seminar.

Also by Jacinth Tracey

Fearless and Fabulous! Workbook
Get Wired2Succeed in Life*
Get Wired2Succeed After Divorce*
Get Wired2Succeed At Work*

*Comprehensive transformation system (includes book,
Workbook, CDs and DVDs)

All products available at: **www.wired2succeed.com**

DUMP YOUR FEAR!

The Complete System for Using Your Mind,
Brain, Body and Spirit to
Overcome Your Fears and
Achieve Your Personal Power

Jacinth Tracey

Wired2Succeed Press
www.wired2succeed.com

Published 2014 by Wired2Succeed Press.

DUMP YOUR FEAR! Copyright © 2014 by Jacinth Tracey. All rights reserved. No part of this publication may be reproduced, stored in a retrieval system or transmitted in any form by any means, electronic, mechanical, photocopying, recording, scanning or otherwise without either the prior written permission of the Publisher, or authorization through payment of the appropriate per-copy fee.

Requests to the Publisher for permission should be addressed to Wired2Succeed, P.O. Box 42397, Vellore PO, Woodbridge, Ontario, Canada, L4H 3M2 or **info@wired2succeed.com.**

Companies, Organizations, Institutions and Industry Publications: Quantity discounts are available on bulk purchases of books for educational purposes, gifts, sponsorships or fundraising.

Cover image © Wired2Succeed.
Cover designed by Jacinth Tracey and Neil Taveres.
Dump Your Fear! is a registered trademark of Jacinth Tracey and Wired2Succeed.

ISBN: **978-0-9936857-0-5**

More Praise for Jacinth Tracey and
Dump Your Fear!

"What a profound revelation! I've never seen anyone talk about cognitive functioning and connecting it to the emotional triggers that help people to transform themselves in quite the same way. It's no surprise to me that Jacinth's motivated the hundreds and hundreds of people she has through her very prestigious career."
>—Pamela Donnelly, author of *How To Be an A+ Parent*

"Jacinth is able to take anyone who's been pre-programmed for failure because of their environment or parental upbringing and turn their lives around. She reveals empowering concepts that will enable you to live a little longer, breathe a little better, make more money and take better care of your children. She transcends your expectations and will begin your life in many cases for the first time."
>—Joel Bauer, author of *How to Persuade People Who Don't Want to Be Persuaded: Get What You Want Every Time!*

"*Dump Your Fear!* is the blueprint for how to overcome your fears, personal limitations and step into your personal power. Jacinth offers a practical guide with easy-to-understand concepts and principles to rapidly get you on the road to success."
>—Monique Bartlett, author of *Kick Start For Weight Loss*

"Absolutely wonderful! Jacinth is able to talk about the extremely complicated topic of cognitive processes and patterns of behavior and break it down into an easy to understand system that puts people back into proper mental health. She really knows her subject."
>—Matt Episcopo, author of *The Power Persuasion System*

.

For being my real life dream-come-true, I dedicate this book to my husband, best friend and kindred spirit, Joee. I am reminded daily of what a blessing you are to me and that our love is truly a gift.

This book is also dedicated to the people and conditions in my life that gave me the opportunity to face my fears head-on and overcome them. They've taught me that it's not the absence of fear that propels one to success; it's the ability to face your fear, control it, and use it to empower yourself. We truly are more powerful than we could ever imagine.

"The whole secret of existence
is to have no fear."
Buddha

"Do that which you fear most, and
the death of fear is certain."
Mark Twain

"Knowing others is intelligence;
knowing yourself is true wisdom.
Mastering others is strength;
mastering yourself is true power."

Tao Te Ching

A Note from the Author

The information contained in this book is not intended to take the place of psychological, psychiatric, medical, or other types of professional services that might be beneficial to anyone seeking to overcome negative life circumstances and dysfunctional thought and behavior patterns. This book is based on my undergraduate studies in experimental psychology, Master's and doctoral studies in the field of mental health; 25 years of professional experience in coaching and performance management of individuals and corporate teams; lessons-learned from specialized training in the power of the subconscious mind, as well as personal life experiences and case studies. Most, if not all, of the information contained in this book has been substantiated by scientific research. Selected references appear at the back of this publication.

In my professional coaching practice, I'm able to guide my clients along the path to overcoming their fear barriers in a very individualized and personalized way. I cannot do this in a book. However, what I can do and what I have done, is to take the essential elements of mindset transformation and behavioral coaching and provide you with helpful and informational material in a way that will shed light into the components of fear and the tools you need to address and overcome fear barriers.

If you're in need of professional medical, psychiatric or other professional advice on a more individual level, I suggest that you seek out a competent professional in that area before adopting the suggestions in the book. I would also invite you to go to my website at **www.wired2succeed.com** and inquire about my coaching and mentoring programs.

Table of Contents

Preface: My Story

"Fear is a darkroom where negatives develop."
Usman B. Asif

"The brave man is not he who does not feel afraid, but he who conquers that fear."
Nelson Mandela

Do you ever wonder why some people stay in friendships, or a dating or marital relationship that they know is bad for them? It's clear to everyone around them that their friend or partner treats them badly, ignores their feelings and would rather keep them down than see them succeed. Sometimes the person is well aware that their relationship is dysfunctional, but they feel trapped and helpless about how to get out of it. Maybe you too have been in that kind of a relationship.

Well, just as we sometimes have dysfunctional relationships with other people, we can also have dysfunctional relationships with ourselves. By that I mean that we keep doing the same things over and over even though the outcomes are rarely what we really want, and in fact, often go against our own best interests. Our head is filled with negative thoughts and we act in ways that practically guarantee that we'll end up with negative results.

We hesitate about every little decision, listening to our set-on-rewind sabotaging inner voice that tells us "You can't do that; You don't know how." or "If you try, you're going make a fool of yourself in front of everyone." or "Don't bother, you'll just be disappointed again." We become paralyzed by fear whenever we even think of moving out of our uncomfortable "comfort zone".

Our fear and the emotions often connected to fear — anger, blame, shame, depression, guilt, and indecision — seem to be beyond our control.

Your fears act like a barrier — a barrier between what you have and what you want; a barrier between the person you are now, and the person you were created to be. Your fears cause you to short-change yourself, and by default, short-change your friends and family because all of your wonderful talents and skills aren't being fully expressed. Your fears cause you to live a fearFULL life of default rather than a fearLESS life of your own design.

I know this story all too well because I lived with fear for much of my life and have worked hard to overcome it. I hardly knew a day when I wasn't afraid of something. My fear wasn't of anything physical mind you. My fear, like most people's fear, was entirely emotional and not a response to any real physical threat or danger. In fact, many of the problems we humans experience in our lives is a function of how we react emotionally to what happens to us, or how we act when we anticipate what may happen to us.

My childhood fears of the "boogieman" gave way to teenage fears of figuring out how best to fit in with friends at school and not knowing how to go about getting what I wanted for my future. During early adulthood my fears changed to those associated with romantic relationships and the financial pressures of putting myself through undergraduate and graduate school. As I matured my fears changed to more spiritual ones; fears that I would leave this world having never discovered the true purpose for my life, my mission, my worthy ideal.

At each stage, I found myself trapped in my own head. I was a prisoner of my own limiting beliefs and habitual responses. It was emotionally and mentally exhausting to be me. Over time I had unknowingly entered into a dysfunctional relationship with fear and it was influencing my thoughts, feelings, actions… and my life outcomes. This relationship kept me in a state of helplessness and limited thinking where I was blinded to the universe of possibilities that was right in front of me.

Thankful for "Aha!" moments

But luckily there were several major "Aha!" moments in my personal and professional life that taught me how to break through my fear barriers and get power and control over my thoughts, feelings and actions. In fact, not only did I learn how to manage my own limiting fears, but the tools I developed allowed me to teach hundreds of other people how to overcome their fear barriers as well. I'll tell you about three of these "Aha!" moments here briefly.

The idea that fear can be effectively managed started peculating in my consciousness during my undergraduate studies in experimental psychology and sociology. Conditioning rats and pigeons in the lab so that they would exhibit specific behaviors as a function of rewards and punishments showed me clearly how behaviors could be programmed, not only for animals, but for us humans as well. My sociology courses showed me that individuality can be a rather vague concept since we're all influenced by the families, cultures and societies that we live in.

I was fascinated by this new knowledge and began to see how I'd been conditioned, and had conditioned myself, into living a life of fear and self-limitation. The fact that I could actually make a conscious decision to re-shape my own thinking and behavior was like seeing a bright light after years spent living in a dark tunnel. I could actually learn to be powerful and optimistic, just as I'd learned to be weak and fearful. I could consciously choose emotions and behaviors that were productive and helpful rather than those that got in the way of my ability to succeed in my personal and professional life.

Another "Aha!" moment occurred during the time I was a doctoral student studying mental health and decided to end my marriage to someone whom I'd been with since I was 21 years-old. We'd spent most of our early adulthood together and, as a result, had many shared memories, friendships and interests. However, in spite of those things, our marriage had grown dysfunctional and emotionally damaging to me and, in my late 30s, I found myself expending much of my mental and emotional energy in an ongoing and mind-numbing stay-or-go debate with myself. I was living the typical "approach-avoidance conflict" that I'd learned about during my undergraduate studies — that is, I was stuck on the fence because the thought of divorcing was equally negative and positive. On the positive side I would get rid of all the stress that came with living in an unhealthy relationship, but the financial burden and severed family ties were definite negatives that cast a shadow over the positives.

But what really held me in place was fear. Fear of the unknown. I'd identified myself as someone's partner or wife for most of my adult life. Who would I be without that role? The thought of leaving the marriage also raised the old familiar fears of my childhood. The fear of feeling unloved (the remnants of abandonment issues caused when my biological father ended all contact with me after he and my mother separated when I was a toddler) and unwanted (caused by a strained relationship with my step-father after my mother remarried) had taken up residence in my mind and was loudly chattering away once again. It kept saying things like "You're in your late 30s; all the good men are taken. You're probably going to end up old and alone." and "You know that this is also going to change your relationship with the friends and colleagues you both have in common, right?"

Although I was extremely unhappy in the marriage, I was afraid of leaving. As a result, I existed in a state of fear, depression, frustration, and anger for years.

But making the decision to end the relationship, even though it opened up a Pandora's Box of financial hardship and broken relationships, turned out to be one of the best decisions of my life. I was able to confront my most debilitating fears and claim my personal power. The strangulation nightmares that I'd been having for years immediately vanished (I later discovered that my subconscious mind had been trying for years to show me that my marriage was figuratively choking the life out of me, but my conscious mind hadn't been ready to accept that fact). I was able to apply the tools and coping strategies I'd been taught in my academic training and the lessons learned from real-life experiences I'd picked up along the way to grow from the experience. In fact, my divorce and my period of self-imposed isolation gave me the opportunity to be alone with my inner world so that I could increase my self-awareness. It became the catalyst for the beginning of my integrating the spiritual connection into the realm of neuroscience (specifically the field of neuroplasticity) and mental health — my own personal life transformation system had begun to emerge.

The third "Aha!" moment happened when, after almost 10 years, I left my corporate executive position to take on entrepreneurship. To some people it might seem foolish for anyone to leave the financial security of a steady six-figure paycheck for the uncharted waters of self-employment. But, my gut instinct and knowledge about the mind-brain-body-spirit connection was telling me that the uneasiness and dissatisfaction that had crept into my professional life was due to the fact that I was experiencing "cognitive dissonance" — a gap between my feelings about the kind of work that I valued and what I was actually doing on my job on a daily basis.

Although I was still actively engaged in my work with its usual 10-12 hour days filled with meetings, managing staff and monitoring their performance, creating and overseeing departmental budgets, etc., organization-wide restructuring had resulted in changes in corporate roles and responsibilities and I no longer had the time to devote to the personal coaching and mentoring of my staff, or even engage with them in any meaningful manner. For me, the ability to help people grow and evolve intellectually, personally and professionally was a key intrinsic reward of my work and a played a significant role in my self-identity and job satisfaction

But there I was, spending most of my waking life engaged in activities that didn't reflect this core value. I knew that I had to make a change to be truly happy and self-fulfilled. However, I encountered an initial fear barrier at the thought of leaving a comfortable salary to start my own business. What if the business wasn't profitable or people didn't want my services? What would I do? I knew for sure that I didn't want to just move from one corporate position to another. Something inside me was driving me; incessantly urging me to venture out on my own. But I had no mentors; no one in my family or immediate social networks had undertaken what I was considering. How was I going to succeed as an entrepreneur with no one to show me what to do?

But once again facing my fear paid off. I decided that my mental and physical health was worth more than job security and made a decision to leave my position. Although to some, it should have been a time of anxiousness and even more fear, I felt surprisingly calm, self-assured and yes ... powerful. I was in control of my own destiny. Within 18 months of leaving my corporate position, I significantly increased my net worth, developed three targeted life transformation systems (i.e., *Get Wired2Succeed in Life; Get Wired2Succeed After Divorce;* and, *Get Wired2Succeed at Work*), published two books and became an internationally-recognized speaker, transformation life coach and mindset mentor.

Loving Life on the other side of Fear

I now spend my time doing what I was meant to do: *teach people how to integrate their mind, brain and body systems and tap into their spiritual energy so that they can successfully move from a fearFULL life to a powerFULL one.* I live authentically; spending my time living my life's mission and doing things that reflect my core values. No more cognitive dissonance. And the icing on the cake was that during that time I also met and married the man of my dreams. I'm certain that the success of my business and marrying my soul mate within months of making the conscious decision to find "the one" came about because I consistently applied my holistic mind-brain-body-spirit life transformation system to every aspect of my personal and professional life and did not let fear get in the way of going after, and getting, the life that I wanted.

The success of my books, webinars and workshops has allowed me to travel internationally, meet a new network of friends and colleagues, and change peoples' lives for the better. I'm able to help my clients in my private coaching practice and hundreds of others through my systematized training tools to overcome their fears and live the life they've always dreamed of but never thought that they could have.

See what can be accomplished when you *Dump Your Fear!*, choose to take control, and embrace your personal power? What if the fears, limiting beliefs and habitual fearful behaviors that are getting in your way of having the life, career, and relationships of your dreams just weren't there anymore? Rest assured that fear doesn't have to be a permanent part of your life.

Trust me and read on. You'll learn that when you *Dump Your Fear*! you'll start to powerfully create the life of your dreams. You'll be able to permanently and consistently live life on your own terms. Don't wait a second longer. Take Control Now!

Introduction

"To conquer fear is the beginning of wisdom."
Bertrand Russell

"The only thing we have to fear is fear itself;
nameless, unreasoning, unjustified terror which paralyzes
needed efforts to convert retreat into advance."
Franklin Delano Roosevelt

If you're frustrated with the lack of progress in your life, then this book is for you. Like most people, the life you're living is probably not what you dreamed about when you were growing up. Back then, you probably had visions of doing something great, meeting interesting people, and having more fun and control over your life. So what happened? Why is it that you're living your life by default, rather than a life of your own design?

Whenever I speak with people, one of the most common complaints I hear is that they're frustrated, angry or depressed about something in their current life circumstances; whether it's in their personal life, their professional life, or both. They're not living the life that they thought they'd be living. Instead, things just seem to have "happened" and they can't really put a finger on how they ended up in the unsatisfying jobs, friendships, relationships, and circumstances that they find themselves. They want things to change, but they fear changing. They also fear staying stuck in the same place, experiencing the same disappointments over and over again and not getting what they want out of life. Their life is full of fear barriers and they're unable to move forward.

1

Fear is at almost epidemic proportions in our society, despite the fact that most of us are quite safe from physical harm on any given day. Our fear is mostly based on how we feel about someone or something, or our perceived ability to deal with that someone or something. For example, we may fear perceived consequences of speaking up for ourselves and so remain silent while being treated disrespectfully or unfairly in our personal or professional relationships. Or we may fear stepping out of our comfort zone and taking on new challenges even though it would allow us to prosper personally, financially, and even spiritually.

We suffocate our true wants, needs and desires under a heavy blanket of fear and end up living a "less than" life because of our fears. As a result, we end up setting a bad example and pass on a fear-based world view to our children who then go on to live fear-based lives themselves. Eventually, we end up leaving this physical world having been less than what we'd been created to be. Just like a report card, our final life grade might state "performed below his/her ability" or "was capable of so much more."

But don't feel bad if you've been living a fearFULL life so far. You're not alone. Fear doesn't discriminate. It affects men and women, the old and the young. It doesn't care about how pretty or handsome you are. It doesn't care about how much money you make, or the color of your skin, or what language you speak. Fear is an opportunist. Let it in, and it'll make itself at home in your internal systems. From that vantage point, it'll take control of all aspects of your life. Next thing you know, fear will be calling the shots in all of your decision-making. You won't be able to make a move without checking in with your fear first.

I've spent the better part of my adult life working in the field of mental and physical health. I've also spent a good chunk of my childhood and adulthood battling some fear barrier or another. So fear, for me, is not just an academic exercise or some abstract concept. Fear is very real. I've seen it play havoc with my mind, my body, and my spirit. I've also seen it in action in the lives of my friends, family, colleagues, employees, clients, and even strangers who choose to share their challenges with me.

Turn FearFULL into FearLESS

But there's good news. You don't have to live a fearFULL life. You can take control and empower yourself to create the life you've always wanted. You can make a conscious decision, starting today, to finally take charge of your life and set the stage for a better future for yourself and those you care about. You *can* kick your fear habit. It doesn't matter how old you are or how much you think you've messed things up in your life. As long as you're living and breathing, you can start to make a change.

I'm a firm believer that it's not how you start this life that matters; it's how you finish. I'm a living testament to that. One of the essential steps necessary to get on the path to success is overcoming fear. Overcoming that little voice in your head that says you "shouldn't" or "can't" do something.

In working through my own issues with fear, I was able to take what I'd learned during my Master's and doctoral studies in mental health, takeaways from specialized training in the power of the subconscious, lessons-learned from 25 years of mentoring individuals and corporate teams in performance management, and my own epiphanies or "Aha!" moments acquired over a lifetime of trial and error, and turn these findings into a proven holistic life transformation system that has worked for me and countless others.

I wanted to give as many people as possible the benefit of what it had taken me decades, and a significant amount emotional pain and money spent in formal education and specialized training, to learn. I didn't want people — like you — to go through all the trial-and-error and time that it took me to finally move from fearFULL to powerFULL. For years I've used my transformation system to guide my life. I've also used it in my teaching, corporate work, and mentoring and coaching practice to successfully help my students, staff, clients and friends push past their fear barriers, get "unstuck", and go after what they want in life.

In my coaching practice I'm able to personally teach my clients, though a process of behavioral modification, systematic desensitization and spiritual awakening, how to break down long-held fear barriers. But there are only so many people that I can coach on an individual basis. So I developed the Wired2Succeed systems (go to **www.wired2succeed.com** for more information) and now this book, to show as many people as possible that no matter how long you've been holding on to dysfunctional thoughts, feelings and behaviors, no matter how long you've lived a life of default rather than a life of your own design, you can indeed rewire your brain, mind and body to create a more powerful and self-directed life.

But I didn't want *Dump Your Fear!* to be scholarly-dry or be perceived as yet another self-help, motivational book that you see lining the shelves in many bookstores. I wanted to teach people — just like you — complicated concepts in mental health, behavioral modification, neuroscience, biology and even spirituality in a way that was informative, accessible and applicable to your own experiences with fear. I share others' experiences and my own personal history of overcoming fear so that you'll see that facing and overcoming your fears isn't so scary after all, and that it can be done if you'll just start with making a committed decision to take control of your fears and your life.

In order to overcome your fear, you first have to understand it. You have to truly get to know it on a personal and intimate level because fear influences you on a personal and intimate level, often without you knowing it. So, in one of my "Aha!" moments I came up with the idea of personifying fear — by making it a "real" person (called Fear) like the people in your own life — rather than teaching about it solely as an abstract psychological concept or theoretical principle.

The people in your life —like your family and close friends — influence you in some way when you interact with them, just like you influence them in some way. Did you ever notice that the more time you spend with someone the more likely you are to take on some of their mannerisms like the way they speak or dress, or even some of their tastes and beliefs? Social psychologists refer to this phenomenon as *social influence.*

Well, guess what? The same thing holds true for Fear; he influences you as well. The more you interact with Fear, the more influence he'll have over your thoughts, your emotions, your behavior…and your results. The same is true for Power; the more you hang around with Power, the more influence he'll have over your thoughts, your emotions, your behavior and your life outcomes. In the same way that your home environment changes depending on who's living there with you, so too does your mental, emotional and spiritual environment change depending on whether you're living in a state of fear or empowerment.

Although we don't always have a choice about interacting with certain people in our family or at work, we do have a choice about whether we live with Fear or with Power. By choosing to live with Power and *Dump Your Fear!*, you'll finally begin to eliminate the dysfunctional thoughts, feelings and behaviors that have kept you from fulfilling your dreams. You'll be able to kick your fear habit once and for all.

Using one of my life transformational systems (known as the *"Three E system"*) I will:

1. **Explain** how you acquired your fears.
2. **Expose** the way fear works in your brain, mind, and body systems.
3. **Elevate** your self-awareness and show you how to achieve unlimited personal power.

By the time you've finished reading *Dump Your Fear!* you'll know how fear operates in your internal systems to keep you living a life of default rather than a life of your own design. You'll know how to identify Fear and the negative influence he has on your thoughts, emotions, behaviors, and life outcomes. You'll know how to acquire the positive influence that Power brings into your life. You'll also know how to use the provided "PowerTools" to rewire your internal systems to ensure that your relationship with Power lasts a lifetime.

I'm so excited to be sharing this book with you and am eternally grateful to all those who've allowed me to show them how to overcome their fear barriers. I feel so blessed when someone shares their success with me and tells me how facing and overcoming their fears has led them to a life beyond what they'd ever imagined — that they have new careers, new relationships and a new, positive outlook about their future. It's my sincere wish that this book will be the catalyst you need to overcome your fears and start living the fearLESS life you were created to live. So now it's your turn. Get ready to *Dump Your Fear!* Don't give into fear and procrastinate any longer. Only you can make the choice to empower yourself now!

To Your PowerFULL Life!

Jacinth Tracey

Chapter One
What is Fear anyway?

"Fear: False Evidence Appearing Real."
Author Unknown

"If you want to know what someone fears, pay close attention to the things they do and listen attentively to the things they say. Fear always reveals its hand."
Jacinth Tracey

"Fear …seems to press on us from within and without, giving constant false testimony".
Marianne Williamson

So, what is fear? Fear is an emotional state. It's a psychological stress response to something or someone (called a *stress trigger* or a *stressor*) that makes you feel threatened. The threat can be real or might exist only in your imagination. Emotional symptoms of fear include anxiety, dread, helplessness, panic, and other types of psychological distress.

Fear has existed since before we climbed out of the primordial ooze as basic life forms. It also existed in the Garden of Eden. Fear is even embedded in our culture and reflected in our superheroes and fairy tales. For example, Superman had a fear — he was afraid of the radioactive element kryptonite, his one weakness — because it sapped his power and could eventually take his life. He feared a *physical* threat. And the wicked queen in the familiar fairy tale Snow White feared not being the most beautiful woman in the land. She was angry and jealous of Snow White's beauty and also feared that with time her own beauty would fade which was her source of power and pride. The source of her threat was *emotional*, but a fear nonetheless. We also often find that fear is a basic ingredient in the storylines of popular movies, cartoons and even video games. It doesn't take a lot of searching to find something in our external environment to reflect fear back at us. So why are we, as individuals and as a society, so preoccupied with and impacted by fear?

It's in your Genes

Like most living and breathing life forms, human beings have been born prewired for fear. Yes, that's right — our ability to experience fear is built right into our genes, it's in our DNA. That's because fear does serve a function. It's part of our survival mechanism. Without fear we wouldn't have survived as a species. We would've been eaten by predators or died because we literally played with fire or suffered some other misadventure. Our fear kept our ancestors alive long enough for them to adapt to hostile environments and give birth to new generations. These new generations acquired the fear trait because it was beneficial to the continued survival of the species.

FEAR FACT #1: Human beings have been born pre-wired for fear. It's a protective mechanism that keeps us from getting hurt.

Because of this, many of the things that cause us to be fearful are deeply ingrained in our brains and have been shaped over millions of years of evolution. For example, you don't have to learn not to walk into a burning building or into a blazing campfire. Something "kicks in" in your brain as you see and feel the flames that prevent you from moving closer to the source of the threat, even before you feel any physical pain or discomfort.

But although fear was initially wired into our genetic makeup by evolutionary forces to be a functional and protective factor in our lives to ensure our survival and the survival of our species, today's fear responses can be quite dysfunctional. In today's modern society, most of our threats don't come in a physical form. There are no wild animals on the prowl in our streets, hostile invaders burning and pillaging our homes, or other physical dangers for us to fear. As such, we don't generally fear for our physical existence. Like the queen in Snow White, most of our fears are emotional or psychological in nature — and that's where the problem lies.

Why is that a problem? It's a problem because of what fear does to us. From a biological and physiological perspective, fear is designed to help us do either of two things: stay and fight, or run away from the threat. It's what's referred to as the *fight-or-flight* response. These responses are pre-wired and patterned, and because of this, our fear responses are quite predictable (i.e., not random). That's right; all human beings (like most species) are creatures of pattern or habit — how we behaved in the past in a particular situation is predictive of how we behave in the present, and how we'll behave in a similar situation in the future.

FEAR FACT #2: When you feel fear it activates your body's *fight-or-flight* arousal system. It's an automatic instinctive reaction to feeling threatened and makes you want to run away from the threat (avoidance) or stay and fight (confrontation).

This predictable, patterned behavior can be a good thing because we don't have to learn from scratch how to react to the same stressor each time. For example, it's a good thing that we only have to learn once how to react to a snarling, angry wild animal. But, our predictable behavior can turn into a bad thing when this behavioral pattern doesn't serve our best interests, or even worse, gets in the way of our ability to adapt successfully to life's challenges. Did you know that it's when we face and overcome life's challenges (that is, when we face and overcome our fears) that we develop and strengthen our sense of mastery and self-esteem which contributes to good mental health? Mastery and self-esteem are important coping mechanisms.

Mastery is when you feel that you're able to control things in your life. *Self-esteem* is the way you think (judgment) and feel (attitude) about yourself in relation to others; it's your emotional evaluation of your own worth. Each time you face and conquer a fear, it improves your ability to cope with similar and other fears in the future because it increases your mastery and self-esteem. But when you habitually think fearful thoughts and react with fear when you're faced with stressors, you actually reinforce and strengthen that fear response in the future. In fact, you actually erode your self-esteem and sense of mastery over yourself and your environment each time you have a fear response.

Let's think of it this way: our patterned thinking and behavior gets wired into our neural makeup and acts like a well-travelled trail that eventually wears a visible neural path into our brain; just like we'd eventually make a noticeable path into a gravel trail if we kept walking over the same area over and over again. Each time we walk over the same places in the gravel trail that we'd previously travelled on, the trail gets smoother and easier to walk on — loose stones don't slip out from under our feet causing our ankles to buckle because we've stamped down the stones into the ground below. As you'll also learn in this book, we also wear an emotional groove into our mind each time we react with fear to an emotional stressor, which also makes it easier for us to remember that we reacted with fear to the same situation on previous occasions.

Each time you give in to fearFULL thoughts and feelings you're travelling down a well-worn gravel trail in your brain and your mind. But not all gravel trails lead to a lovely scenic view where you're excited to find that even more beautiful scenery lies beyond the horizon. The gravel trail made by fear leads to an imposing brick wall where your view of anything beyond where you stand is obstructed. You can't see a thing except for that huge, imposing wall — your *fear barrier* — in front of you. Each time you think a fearFULL thought and give into your fears, you're putting another brick into your wall; you're strengthening your fear barrier. Give into your fears often and long enough and you'll eventually build a fear barrier that you'll come to believe is insurmountable.

The Element of Choice

But did you know that you have a *choice* about whether or not you react fearFULLy or fearLESSly to situations in your life? Well, you do. Although coming face-to-face with certain things or situations may cause you to initially experience fear, there's a lot of room to maneuver in terms of your potential conscious thoughts, feelings and reactions. That's because of the nature of stressors as well as our own human nature.

Stressors are situations, things or people in our environment that we perceive to be challenging or threatening. When we encounter a stressor, this triggers a reaction or a stress response. *There are many types of stressors and many types of stress responses; fear is just one type of stress response.* Stress is easier to tolerate if it's predictable, positive and we feel that we have some control over the situation. That type of stress can actually be good for us because it drives us to succeed and keeps us alert and motivated — such as when athletes compete in an event. On the other hand, stress is harder to take if we view it as negative, we weren't expecting it, and we don't think we have any control over what happens to us. This is particularly the case when the stress trigger causes us to feel fear.

Take the example of what could happen as you drive along a highway. Let's say that you're driving at normal speed on the highway and the car in front of you breaks suddenly for no apparent reason (a stress trigger). You might immediately feel one or more stress-related emotion including fear, anxiety, or even anger as you try to slow down your own vehicle in time to avoid a collision. In any event, this reaction to the stress trigger causes you to take action (take your foot off the gas and apply the brake) so that you avoid an accident.

In the example above, almost everyone would agree that having the car in front of you on a highway suddenly break for no reason, causing you to slam on your breaks, is something negative and unpredictable. As such, a short-lived fear response is reasonable — the fear response caused by the stressor is a good thing. The response in fact alerted you to danger and you took action to avoid a collision, potentially saving you from physical harm. However, not all stressors are so clear-cut. In fact, not everyone agrees that some things or situations are stressful at all.

FEAR FACT #3: Fear is just one of the ways that you can react emotionally to a stress trigger.

Take black cats as an example. In some cultures, like Canada, the United States and parts of Europe, black cats are viewed as negative — don't let a black cat cross your path or you'll get bad luck. But, in other cultures, like Britain and Japan, black cats are viewed positively and are in fact perceived to bring good luck. The black cat itself has no power as a stress trigger;

it's the culture's *collective* interpretation of what the black cat means that has the power to cause fear, as well as the *individual* interpretation of the person in the path of the black cat. In the United States and Canada, a person fearing that a black cat is about to cross her path might take evasive action to get out of the path of the black cat. But in Japan, she would feel no fear, and in fact might well alter her pace to ensure that the black cat does indeed cross her path.

> **FEAR FACT #4**: The way you respond to things, people and situations is based on your perception of whether or not they are stressors.

Let's take another example. Say there are three people on the top floor in a high-rise office building and they hear a fire alarm go off. One person might wonder calmly whether it's a false alarm or if the alarm is being tested. The second person might feel a bit anxious but might also first look around for cues to see how others are responding to the alarm before taking any action. But the third person might jump to the conclusion that the fire is real and, not only that, but that the fire is raging out of control. The trigger for all three reactions is the same: the fire alarm going off. When the alarm went off, each of them stopped what they were doing and focused on it. But it's how the alarm was *interpreted* that makes the difference. In the first two examples, the stress trigger caused the person to pay attention but there was no fear associated with it. In the last example, the interpretation that the fire alarm must mean that the building is ablaze caused a definite fear reaction.

How someone reacts to a stressor is generally based on the type of stressor, how long they've been dealing with the stressor, their previous experiences (particularly their childhood experiences), their personal beliefs (particularly about their ability to cope with the stressor) and even their genetic predisposition. Because of that, people's reaction to the same situation can vary quite a bit. How we react emotionally to life circumstances based on our perceptions and interpretations of them have significant consequences for our ability to overcome our fear barriers and succeed in our life.

Chapter Two
What causes Fear?

"Nothing in life is to be feared. It is only to be understood."
Marie Curie

"Fear is a question: What are you afraid of, and why? Just as the seed of health is in illness, because illness contains information, your fears are a treasure house of self-knowledge if you explore them."
Marilyn Ferguson

You now know that the ability to experience fear is part of your genetic inheritance; that it's been pre-wired into your DNA to help you survive from primarily physical threats. It's innate or natural. But guess what? Not all fears are innate. In fact, most of the things we humans fear have nothing to do with our innate fear for our physical survival. So what happened? What happened is that *we learned our fears*. That's right, we learned to be fearFULL.

Some of the fears that people report most frequently are:
- Fear of being alone
- Fear of social rejection or ridicule
- Fear of public speaking
- Fear of failure
- Fear of success
- Fear of speaking up or asserting yourself
- Fear of losing control
- Fear of intimacy
- Fear of not having enough money

- Fear of the future
- Fear of moving on from a current job or relationship
- Fear of one's own death or the death of a loved one
- Fear of sickness, serious illness or injury
- Fear of aging
- Fear of heights
- Fear of flying
- Fear of making decisions
- Fear of the unknown

Are you struggling with one or more of these fears? Are they presenting a barrier between the person you are now and the person you'd like to become? You're not alone. Most people have fear barriers — some aspect of their personal or professional life that they'd like to change but seem unable to because of their fears. Like you, their fear is keeping them from moving on and experiencing a better, more fulfilling life.

Learning to Fear

When you take a look at the list above, or think of another fear you can add to the list, it's likely that you'll see that the thing you fear isn't something physical or environmental at all; your fear is about something emotional or psychological. And to make matters worse, you learned these fears; you weren't born with them.

FEAR FACT #5: Most of your fears are learned and are not an innate or natural part of who you are.

Most of what we fear was learned along the way through our direct personal experience with a source of threat, or by watching or finding out about someone else's experience with the threat.

This process is called *conditioning*. When we learn how to feel and behave from interacting with our environment or by observing the behavior of others, we're being conditioned to feel and behave in a particular way. Conditioning causes us to develop thoughts and behavioral habits based on experience, not by instinct.

The conditioning of emotional responses, like fear, is well documented in the behavioral sciences. In fact, in order to earn my Bachelor of Science degree in experimental psychology (an area of psychology that uses scientific methods to research the brain functioning and associated behavior of humans and animals) I had to condition rats and pigeons so that they'd display certain behaviors, like pecking a specific button or avoiding a certain part of their cage. This required lab component of my studies taught me not only how to condition these animals, but how to shape and modify their behavior once they were conditioned. By applying my knowledge of stimulus-response and reinforcement contingencies, I was able to see first-hand the effect of conditioning on motivation, thought patterns, attention, learning, memory and perception.

Most introductory psychology classes teach about conditioning and the ease with which not only animals, but human beings, can have their behavior shaped or conditioned. Take the famous Pavlovian experiment in classical conditioning for example. Pavlov's experiment involved him pairing the ringing of a bell with the presentation of food (called a *stimulus*) to a dog. Whenever the dog saw the food he'd salivate (called the *response*) because he anticipated the delicious taste of the food. In the experiment, moments before Pavlov fed the dog, he'd ring a bell. Soon the dog learned that when he heard the bell that meant that he'd be getting fed. The sound of the bell alone eventually became enough to get the dog to salivate. The bell became the new stimulus, not just the actual food. The dog had been conditioned to expect food whenever he heard the bell and so had a habitual behavioral response even before he even saw the food.

We humans learn our fear response to many things in pretty much the same way. That is, at some point we had a fear reaction to something and now just the thought of that thing can evoke a fear response. We have a conditioned response because we previously made an association between two things (the stressor and our fear response). For example, have you ever started salivating even before you took the first bite of your meal? You haven't put the food in your mouth; your taste buds haven't made any contact with the food. Yet you begin to salivate simply by anticipating the delicious taste of your meal. That's because, on previous occasions, you enjoyed your meal and this pleasant memory has been wired into your internal brain, mind and body systems. This same "anticipatory" process is also responsible for wiring unpleasant fearful memories into your internal systems causing you to have a fear reaction to physical and emotional stress triggers that may not even be present at the time you're having a fear response. We're no different from Pavlov's dog; we're easily conditioned.

Learning from personal .experience (direct conditioning)

We often condition ourselves without even knowing it. At some point along the way, something or some event in our life caused us to associate it with a threat or danger. Our direct experience of this threat activated our fight-or-flight arousal response and now we have that negative association in our head. Because this association has "stuck", the fear we have about that thing or event triggers our fight-or-flight response just by thinking about it. So now we're motivated to avoid that stress trigger and we never give ourselves the chance to test out whether our initial reaction to it was valid or not. This is the way our fear becomes a habit.

Let's take an example. As a child Anne was stung by a bee (stimulus) while playing in the yard. The bee sting hurt and she cried and ran back inside the house (response). This reduced the physical threat because, after all, the bee wasn't going to chase her back into the house. By fleeing from the bee she removed the threat. The next time Anne was in the yard and a bee flew by, she remembered the pain of that bee sting because she'd made an association between bees and pain. Seeing a bee is now a stimulus or stress trigger; it presents a threat of being stung and automatically activates Anne's fight-or-flight response.

But that's a problem because each time Anne sees a bee she's automatically put into fight-or-flight mode; regardless of whether or not the bee even comes near her. Anne's fear of bees has become a habit, and avoidance of bees has become a habitual stress response. Even though she was only stung once, in her entire life, Anne perceives bees as a threat. After that first sting, she never put herself in a situation to test out whether or not bees would "always" sting her (which they won't). The false belief and anticipation that they will sting her is enough to make her feel fear and react with avoidance. This avoidance can have a cascading effect in that Anne might tend to avoid other things that could be associated with bees; like barbeques and picnics, walks in the park, or outdoor concerts. In the end, the primary source of Anne's fear (that is, bees) cascades or spills over into other areas of her life that aren't sources of threat in themselves.

We learn our fears from our direct experiences but we can learn our fears from our indirect experiences as well. For example, some children are raised in households where their father or mother demands perfection from them, and perhaps even withholds love or affection if they feel that the child fell short in some way. If the child fails to score a goal during a baseball game or get all A's on his report card, for example, the parent may show their disappointment or disapproval by telling the child that he's "less than" or become emotionally distant for a period of time. The child is therefore conditioned and makes an association between being perfect and being loved or accepted.

Over time, the child's sense of how worthy he is as a person becomes deeply associated with doing things perfectly. Falling short in any way makes him feel worthless and a "loser". His sense of self-worth is tied up with how well he performs and he eventually becomes his own worst critic. He judges himself more quickly and more harshly than anyone else would ever judge him. So even if he appears to be competent and successful to other people, he might secretly have a fear of failure or a fear of being rejected that effects his ability to truly enjoy his accomplishments.

> **FEAR FACT #6**: You learn (are conditioned) to fear certain things or situations through your own direct personal experience. This applies to physical threats as well as emotional threats.

Learning by observing others
(indirect conditioning)

But we don't always acquire our fears through our direct experience with stressors or threats; sometimes we acquire fears simply by observing other people. As we interact with our environment we're also interacting with and learning from others. We can learn to fear certain things or situations simply by observing their reactions to certain things or situations. We become influenced by other people and adopt their attitudes and expectations. In that way, we can also adopt the same fear responses they have — a process referred to as *social fear learning* or *social fear conditioning*.

From the day we're born, the first social influences that we encounter come from our immediate family unit. Our mother, father, sisters and brothers are the first and closest social influences on our lives. In fact, before we become teenagers and begin to think more independently and want to have our own opinions and preferences, our family is the most important source of social influence on our emotional development. They influence our self-image and shape our tastes, our values, our attitudes, our behaviors... and yes, even our fears.

Because our families are very powerful influencers, seeing their fearful reactions to things, people and situations often causes us to fear the same or similar things, people and situations. If we'd been raised by ourselves, without that negative influence, it's unlikely that we'd have these fears. What's worse is that when we grow up and have children of our own, we end up transferring these same fears to them unless we make a conscious effort to stop the cycle. Social learning is how things like family traditions, as well as political affiliations and various types of prejudice are passed down from generation to generation. It's like when you program or install software on a computer — the same software program can be downloaded from one computer to another and can even be replicated across an endless number of computers with no modification from the original program. In this way the computer program stays intact, just like fears can stay intact.

Research shows that social conditioning is real and has significant effects on how people learn to think and behave. For example, there's scientific evidence to show that areas of the brain that get activated when we personally experience fear are the same areas of the brain that get activated when we see someone else experience fear. In other words, our brain gets conditioned whether we're experiencing the stressor ourselves or if we're simply just observing someone else experiencing it. Conditioning is a powerful thing.

Let's take a silly but appropriate example of conditioning or social learning. My sister dislikes peas. She doesn't like their texture or the way they taste. For as long as I can remember she's picked the peas off her plate whenever my mother served them to us with dinner when we were growing up. I have my own food preferences and dislikes as well. For example, I dislike celery because of the stringy fibers and always peel my peaches because I dislike the "fuzzy" taste of their skins, although I like the taste of the fruit itself.

When my sister married and had her first child I noticed that some of the baby food she served was in fact peas. My niece would sit in her high chair and eat those mushy peas with no protest; in fact it looked like she really enjoyed them. But as my niece left babyhood behind and became a toddler, I noticed that she'd changed her view on peas; that she was in fact picking them off her plate with her tiny fingers or pushing them to the side like her mother did. What had happened to her enjoyment of peas?

Well, wanting to be a big girl like her mommy, my niece had started to model the pea-hating behavior of my sister. Never once did my sister tell her young daughter that she should start disliking peas just like she did. My niece, like all humans and other higher order species, had learned from interacting with and observing her social environment. Her tastes were being shaped by others, as are all our tastes, values, beliefs and attitudes.

Sometimes the things we learn from our family aren't quite as trivial as a dislike of peas or celery. For example, I once worked with a colleague who had a fear of driving on the highway. Part of our work on the Alzheimer's disease study we were conducting involved visiting the home of our 200 study participants every two months. During these visits we'd conduct psychiatric, medical and social assessments of the patients, and also assess the safety of their living situation and measure the level of caregiver stress.

While I would travel to the patients' homes using the highway, when it was her turn to visit the family, my colleague would use side roads and the occasional main street. My travelling time was a fraction of her travelling time. Over the two-year study she must have logged hundreds of miles more than I did. When I asked her why she had such a fear of driving on the highway, she told me that her mother had a fear of driving on the highway. As a child, being in the car with a fearful, nervous mother at the wheel caused her to feel anxious herself and had conditioned her own fear of driving on the highway. She knew that this fear was costing her time, gas money, and extra wear-and-tear on her car but couldn't bring herself to confront this fear. She couldn't envision herself driving on the highway even though she knew that it would make her life easier. Until she made the conscious decision to change things by taking control of her fear, her conditioning remained intact.

This conditioning is the same for all humans and all social animals. For example, monkeys learn how to survive in the wild by looking to see how others in their group survive. So, if a monkey sees the members of his group run away when they see a predatory cat, it runs away too. The monkey doesn't have to have direct encounter with the predator and risk getting killed and eaten; it can learn to avoid this threat by watching and benefitting from the experience of other monkeys in his group.

This natural ability to learn by simply observing others, without having to experience the consequences of the threat ourselves, makes perfect sense when we think about physical or environmental threats. It's a good thing that we don't all have to learn for ourselves to fear certain things or situations that could put us in real physical danger. But when we take on the emotional fears of other people through social fear learning, then that natural ability to learn by observation becomes maladaptive for us. It can cause us to develop fears we wouldn't otherwise have.

How you've come to fear certain situations and things is caused by conditioning — how you've conditioned yourself, and the conditioning you received from your family. In essence, the person you are is not self-made. None of us are self-made. The family we were raised in plays a crucial role in how we all think, feel and behave; much of the time without us even knowing it.

FEAR FACT #7: Many of your fears come from your early childhood conditioning, particularly by your family. They can condition or program you for fear.

But, guess what? Our family aren't the only ones who influence or condition us. As we go through life we're constantly being conditioned every day of our lives. The friends we interact with, the movies and television shows we watch, the songs we listen to, the video games we play, and even the books and magazines we read all play a role in our ongoing fear learning and social conditioning. The messages we take in as a function of this interaction help to determine how we see ourselves, and whether we think we can control what happens to us. Most of the time we don't even know that this conditioning is happening and how much it's affecting us and our self-concept.

For example, it's no secret that there are hundreds of magazines and television shows depicting "beautiful" people, their luxury lifestyles and their expensive possessions. We're bombarded with images like this on an almost daily basis. In fact, we take in so much of that information that some of us might begin to judge our own life in a negative light.

You might ask yourself: Why don't I have the same nice things? What's wrong with me? Why aren't I as handsome or as pretty? Why aren't I as skinny? Why don't I have washboard abs or perfect teeth? Will I ever be able to get more than what I currently have? This social comparison can lead to various fears based on your self-esteem and sense of self-worth. For example, you may develop a fear of being judged or rejected; a fear of failure; or a fear of the future because you don't feel that you're capable of getting expensive things like they have or looking like they do.

FEAR FACT #8: The people and things you encounter in your environment, including the media, also condition or program you. They can create fear and other negative emotions by influencing how you feel about yourself.

Conditioning is the root cause for why there's so much variation in fears among people. What some people fear, others embrace. For example, some people have a paralyzing fear of dogs, while others have them in their homes as beloved and valuable members of their family. Some people enjoy riding on roller coasters while others have an intense fear of heights or of falling. Some people love public speaking and take every opportunity to be the centre of attention, while others hide from the spotlight and feel fear at the very thought of having to be at the front of a room speaking to a crowd of people. Some people look to the future with anticipation and hope while others look to the future with fear and dread. What you fear says a great deal about how you've been conditioned throughout your life and your thoughts about your ability to overcome fear barriers.

Identifying the trigger

But the good news is that once you're aware that you've been conditioned for fear you can begin to think for yourself. Decide for yourself if you like peas or celery or driving on the highway or if you want washboard abs. The key to overcoming your conditioning, and your fears, is to understand their source and how they impact you. You're in charge of your own self-image no matter how conditioned by others and your environment you've become. Don't let other people or your previous experiences put limits on what you can do in the future. You have control over how you see yourself and what happens to you.

Ask yourself some of these questions about your fear or fears:

1. What causes me to feel fearFULL?
2. What am I doing or not doing in my life that is evidence of this fear(s)?
3. Where do I think that fear(s) came from?
4. Did it come from my own direct experience, or did I learn it by seeing someone else experience it or by hearing about it?
5. How have I maintained and reinforced this fear(s) over time?
6. How has that fear(s) affected my life in the past and in the present?
7. On a scale of 1-10 (with 1 being "not very disruptive to my personal/professional life" and 10 being "very

disruptive to my personal/professional life") how would I rate this fear(s)?

8. How would I feel if I didn't have this fear(s)?
9. How would I act if I didn't have this fear(s?
10. What could my personal relationships be like if I didn't have this fear(s)? What options might open up for me?
11. What could my professional life be like if I didn't have this fear(s)? What options might open up for me?

How did you do with the questions on this list? Did you find that you had more than one fear? If you did, rank them; placing what you fear most at the top of the list with the other fear(s) below it so that your list runs from what you fear most to what you fear least. This will give you a visual cue as to the fear that troubles you the most and perhaps what you should focus on while you read this book. The more you can confront your fear and imagine what your life would be like without it, the more motivated you'll be to make the necessary changes. This is the first step toward breaking down your fear barriers.

Knowing exactly what you're afraid of and how it impacts your personal and/or professional life is the first step towards moving from fearFULL to fearLESS. Now that you've identified your fear or fears, it's time to put it into context and determine what type of stress triggers you're reacting to and what it's doing to your brain, mind and body. Once you know that, you can take an additional step forward towards addressing and dumping your fear once and for all.

Acute versus Chronic stressors

Because we're all social beings, a significant amount of our stress comes from how we're affected by our environment (including the people and situations we encounter). In other words, our external social environment has a lot of influence over our internal emotional environment. Things such as how we've been raised, how our family, friends, co-workers and strangers treat us, and the numerous roles we have to assume on a day-to-day basis (such as wife or husband, daughter or son, sister or brother, mother or father, employee or boss, caregiver or dependent, etc.) can all be a source of stress for us and contribute to our fears.

We get a lot of information about how we feel about ourselves and our ability to cope from interacting with our social environment. When we don't feel that we have the ability to cope, that feeling of emotional "overload" can activate a fear response. For example, if your boss gives you an important assignment and you don't think that you're capable of handling the workload or don't have the skills necessary to do a good job, you might have an automatic fear response to this request.

Whenever you feel fear, you're experiencing stress. That's because fear is an emotional response to a perceived threat or stressor. *A stressor is the thing, person or situation and stress is what you feel as a result of being exposed to the stressor.* Most physical stressors that cause us to feel fear are short-lived and infrequent; that is, they don't come into our life and stick around for a long period of time. They are what we call *acute* stressors. However, it's often the opposite case for emotional stressors. These stressors tend to not be in a hurry to go anywhere, and can go on and on for days, weeks, months, years ... even a lifetime. We call these *chronic* stressors.

There's a significant difference in the effect of acute and chronic stressors, just like in the case of acute and chronic illnesses. Acute illnesses, like when you get a cold or the flu, only last for a little while. You usually get over a cold or flu within 1-2 weeks. But chronic illnesses like diabetes or asthma tend to stick around for years, or even a lifetime.

Acute Stressors	Chronic Stressors
• Your boss can't attend a Board meeting later that afternoon and asks you to give his written report to the group.	• Your boss tells you that you're required to give reports to the Board as part of your new job responsibilities.
• Your overbearing in-laws are coming for an afternoon visit.	• Your overbearing in-laws are moving in with you permanently.
• You are passing through a war zone.	• You live in a war zone and have no options to relocate.

With chronic stressors, like chronic illnesses, we get a prolonged exposure to something that affects us physically and/or emotionally. This keeps our bodies in a constant state of activation as we live in a near-constant state of fight-or-flight due to the perceived threat. Living with chronic stressors means that we have stress hormones constantly circulating through our internal system which causes us to become chronically stressed. This situation is not good for us because it eventually leads to wear and tear and sometimes a breakdown in parts of our internal system.

FEAR FACT #9: Fear is a form of stress. It can either be acute (short-term) or chronic (long-term) in duration.

Chronic stress and our physical health

Research has shown that living with chronic stress can lead to physical problems such as heart disease, strokes, allergies, high blood pressure, stomach problems, headaches, muscle tension, shallow breathing, and even emotional issues such as anxiety, depression and panic attacks. Some have even gone so far to say that chronic stress can also increase the risk for various types of cancers and that almost all illnesses and diseases and have a stress-based component. When we get exposed to chronic stressors we can eventually end up with health issues that are often more chronic and serious than the original stressor itself.

Let's take an example of the chronic stress I experienced before I left my corporate position that I talked about in the Preface. For about a year-and-a-half, as my corporate role evolved and the fast-paced work environment that I'd been used to for almost a decade sped up exponentially, I began to notice that I was growing increasingly dissatisfied with my role. Initially I did experience a fear reaction to the cognitive dissonance and uncertainty, but once I made a decision about what I intended to do, and formulated a plan of action, the fear dissipated (as you'll learn in later chapters, gaining a sense of control over your life outcomes is a great way to confront your fears).

Like most corporate executives, I was aware that chronic stress usually went with the territory of making a high salary; after all we have budgets and people to manage and corporate projects to deliver often within a short timeframe. But I figured that I could handle the increasing stress for as long as I remained in my position given that I was vigilant about applying good coping skills. With my positive mental outlook, toolkit of coping skills and determination to terminate the stressor (my job) as soon as possible, I imagined that I could be an exception to the rule and would escape the negative effects of chronic stress...or so I thought.

For the first few months all was well. I focused on the remaining parts of my work that I still enjoyed and successfully battled any negative thoughts that would pop up during the days and evenings by replacing them with positive ones. But as time wore on, I found that I wasn't able to apply as many of the coping tools that I would have liked. For example, working for 10-12 hours a day meant that I left work too late to attend my much-loved 6:30PM yoga class. The lack of physical exercise and reduction in time to relax and meditate, combined with hours of sitting at my desk or in meetings, meant that stress hormones were allowed to accumulate in my system. Scheduled back-to-back cross-functional team meetings throughout the day meant that I had to skip lunch many times a week or hurriedly grab a bite on the way from one meeting room to another. That meant that my body wasn't getting the right amount of nutrition and I was prone to fatigue. Moreover, because I left work late in the evenings my mind wouldn't shut off when I went to bed at night and my sleep was disturbed. The lack of sleep, particularly NREM sleep when the body repairs and regenerates tissues and shores up the immune system, meant that despite my coping methods, my physical and mental health were becoming compromised.

Before long I noticed that I was getting stomach aches and other types of abdominal pain. The pains and abdominal bloating, which were intermittent at first, became a daily occurrence and I eventually had to seek medical help when over-the-counter remedies stopped working. After being initially misdiagnosed for months with lactose intolerance and irritable bowel syndrome, I was eventually correctly diagnosed as having over 15 food allergies — allergies that I didn't have the year before. I was placed on a very limited diet to cleanse my system (which was difficult since most of the items like eggs, milk, yeast, wheat, and cane sugar were found in many foods) and advised to reduce my exposure to stress until my body could heal itself.

I couldn't believe it! With all my specialized training and determination I hadn't escaped the powerful effects of living with chronic stress. Rushing from one meeting to another with little or no time to eat, handling multiple demands on my time and energy, having little sleep and responding to an ever-evolving corporate portfolio, had led to an accumulation of stress hormones in my body to a point where it led to real physical consequences.

Let's take another example. Last year I ran into the sister of a long-time friend in a department store while shopping for items for my new home. As we caught each other up on recent events, I told Elaine that I'd followed my instincts, changed careers and that I was finally living the life I'd always envisioned for myself. While I was telling her about the chronic stress I'd experienced during the last year of my employment and the new allergies I'd acquired, Elaine interrupted me with news of her own.

To my surprise she opened the top button on her blouse to show me a large vertical scar running down the middle of her chest. She then told me that not only had she suffered a heart attack two years earlier, but had had two aneurisms caused by being under constant chronic stress at work; particularly due to the unreasonable demands of a harsh and critical boss. Elaine was now on paid medical leave and was planning to go back to university to re-educate herself so that she wouldn't have to return to the job that had almost taken her life. She told me about how her heart attack had frightened her teenage son and her husband and they'd feared losing a mother and wife who was only in her mid-40's.

FEAR FACT #10: Physical health problems can result from being under chronic stress (such as habitually responding to stressors with fear).

As she told me her story I couldn't help but think about my own recent run-in with chronic stress in the workplace. I'd escaped with a few allergies but she'd barely escaped with her life. But the reality is that Elaine and I are not alone. Unfortunately, the situation that we found ourselves in is experienced by millions of people. Studies conducted in the United States, Canada and Europe find that men and women who work in highly stressful jobs or work for "bad bosses" tend to be at higher risk for cardiovascular and heart disease (including heart attack) than people in the general population. Although, in some studies, the risk drops a bit when other risk factors are taken into account (for example, a person's level of income, and lifestyle choices such as what they eat and if they exercise regularly), it's clear that the chronic stress caused by job strain, like most chronic stress, puts a strain on the body that can lead to serious health consequences.

Although people differ in how they respond to chronic stressors, research shows that continued exposure to these stressors is bad for our physical well-being because of the burden it places on our system. That's because we're designed to respond to short-term acute physical or environmental threats, not long-term chronic emotional or psychological threats. Living with chronic stress keeps us in a state of physiological fight-or-flight arousal with little opportunity for our bodies to relax and rid ourselves of the stress hormones.

Chronic stress and our mental health

Exposure to chronic stressors not only puts us at risk for physical health problems, it increases our risk for mental health problems as well. Let's take Alison as an example. I met a man who'd gone through a nasty and contentious divorce a few years earlier. After a bitter and costly custody battle, his ex-wife took their children (aged 17, 21 and 10 years) to live with her in another country.

Although Alison's mother remarried shortly after the divorce, she remained bitter and angry towards her ex-husband. Alison was the youngest of her siblings and didn't understand the divorce. She only knew that her life had changed; that the relationship between her parents had changed, and that she was now being raised by a step-father who didn't seem to like her very much, and that her biological father was now living with another woman and raising another child.

Soon after they relocated, Alison's older siblings, and her only immediate source of social support, moved out of her mother's house leaving her the only child left at home. Because she had no other children at home and was fearful of Alison's continued emotional attachment to her father, her mother grew increasingly domineering and controlling towards Alison. She regulated her every move and even chose the clothes she was allowed to wear. She also began to use Alison as an emotional weapon against her ex-husband. Not only did she make it difficult for him to get access to Alison, but she kept up a near-constant barrage of negative talk against him, reminding Alison of how he'd abandoned his own family to have a child with another woman whom she despised.

This ongoing negative talk against her father was an additional chronic stressor for Alison. Whenever she was on the phone with him, her mother would be on the other line the entire time and would interrupt their conversation with nasty comments about him and his new relationship. Whenever Alison did get the opportunity to visit her father, her mother would phone her numerous times a day demanding an account of the day's activities and remind Alison that he was a bad father and really didn't love her because he'd abandoned her and the family to start a new life with another woman. The "I'm the victim" attitude that the father assumed after the divorce was also a source of stress for Alison because it played on her sympathies and denied her the opportunity to express her anger towards him for leaving the family for fear of hurting his feelings.

During her yearly visits to see her father I'd sometimes get the opportunity to meet with Alison to see how she was doing. Although she expressed a desire to leave her dysfunctional home environment so she could stay with her father and get counseling from me, she was afraid of her mother's reaction. And so, despite gaining some degree of personal control over her life during her visits, she'd return to an environment that pulled her back down into a sense of learned helplessness and repressed anger. Alison felt torn between her two parents and was unable to assert any real control over her life.

Over the years the chronic stress and inability to have control over her own life took a toll on Alison. At first she developed severe acne (sudden skin disorders are one of the signs that someone may be under stress) and later developed a serious eating disorder. She had her first hospitalization for anorexia when she was barely 15 years old. The mother blamed the father's actions and the father blamed the mother's actions for Alison's condition. By the time she was 20 years old, Alison had been in rehab for anorexia and alcohol abuse several times. Each time she completed rehab, she returned to her mother's house to the same situation and the ongoing push and pull between her biological parents.

Eventually Alison was able to leave her dysfunctional home environment by going against her mother's wishes and attending a college thousands of miles away. However the emotional damage had been done. Alison would relapse with episodes of anorexia and alcohol abuse several more times while she was away at school, particularly when she felt that she couldn't cope with certain types of acute stress in her personal relationship with her friends or boyfriend. To this day Alison, now in her late-20's, is fighting an ongoing battle with anorexia and alcohol abuse.

Alison spent most of her life living in a state of chronic stress. She continually felt torn and anxious about her mother's insistence that she sever ties with her father and was made to feel helpless because of her mother's overbearing and controlling behavior. She was fearful about angering or disappointing the mother she loved and internalized her fears and negative feelings to the extent that they showed up as anorexia and alcohol abuse and dependency. Although the divorce itself was no doubt a stressful life event for Alison, it was the years of living with chronic parental stress that eventually took a toll on her mental health and well-being.

FEAR FACT #11: Mental health problems can result from being under chronic stress (such as habitually responding to stressors with fear).

So, as we've seen, chronic stress can have a profound impact of peoples' lives. It can lead to physical as well as emotional problems if not properly addressed. Because *fear is a form of stress*, that means that it too can be acute (short-lived) or chronic (recurring on ongoing).

When we have a short-lived reaction to a stressor, we quickly get our minds and bodies back to a relaxed state. But did you know that when you habitually react with fear to stressors it acts in much the same way as a prolonged exposure to chronic stress? That's right. When you react with fear to life circumstances and have fearful thoughts and feelings for days, weeks, months or even years, you're actually living with chronic stress; just as you'd be living with chronic stress if you were working at a stressful job or living in a stressful relationship for a long time. *Experiencing fear, even at low levels on an ongoing or recurring basis puts you at risk for the same mental and physical health consequences that exposure to chronic stress does.*

Directing our focus to just the stressors themselves, however, won't give us the complete picture about why we experience fears or how we can overcome them. Although they do provide some important clues, we can't pay attention only to what exists outside ourselves to find the answers to our fear questions. To find those answers, we must also look inside ourselves; to what makes us tick. That's because much of the way we respond to stressors occurs within our internal brain, mind and body systems; well below our level of conscious awareness. It's only when we begin to determine how specifically our internal life interacts with what's happening in our external life that we begin to know who we are and why we do the things we do.

Chapter Three
Overview: Fear Gets in Our Systems

"What we think of as our reality is really just the interplay between our internal and external systems."
Jacinth Tracey

"Is the system going to flatten you out and deny you your humanity, or are you going to be able to make use of the system to the attainment of human purposes?"
Joseph Campbell

"A car can't operate without the mechanical systems working, but it can operate with a few dents and scratches…, you are the same."
Mike Dolan

Did you know that everything in our entire world consists of internal and external systems? A system is defined as a set of separate things working cooperatively together as a complex whole to perform a common function. The idea of *function* is an important one when we're talking about any system. That's because each part of a system has a unique function, and in order for the entire system to function properly, each of its component parts need to function properly. Whenever there's a breakdown in any one of the system components, the overall system can't function as well as it should, or may not even function at all.

Let's take a simple audiovisual system as an example. At a minimum, it usually consists of speakers, amplifiers, and a CD or DVD player. Each component of the system has a unique function but really can't do much on its own. You need to use all three together or you won't be able to listen to music or watch your favourite movie. If say, the DVD component of your audiovisual system is working but the speakers fail to function properly, you might be able to watch a movie, but you wouldn't be able to hear any sound — you wouldn't be able to hear what the actors were saying or be moved emotionally by the theme music. Watching the movie this way would result in a "less than" experience and your overall feeling about how good the movie was would be reduced. It's the same way with your life. Just like your cell phone or your computer has operating systems, you also have *internal* operating systems that need all of its components working effectively together to allow you to function to the best of your ability. If you go through life only using some components of your internal systems rather than using them all to their maximum ability, you'll get a "less than" life with "less than" results. We'll talk more about how our mind, brain, body and spirit are components of our internal systems in a bit. Right now let's focus on our external systems.

Our *external systems* are made up of physical and social systems. An example of a physical system is the ecosystem we live in which includes the plants, animals and even the air we breathe. We also live in social systems — groups of people who interact with and mutually influence each other's thoughts and behaviors. For example, our families are a social system, and so are our friends, our workplaces, the communities we live in, and even society in general.

External systems, particularly social systems help to define who we are and how we feel about ourselves. That's because, we can't help but be influenced by the social systems that we operate in. Even though we're all unique individuals, we can't help but be influenced psychologically and emotionally by the social systems in our lives. For example, you've now learned that you've been directly and indirectly conditioned for fear just simply by living and interacting with your family and your wider social environment. The collective influences of these social systems helped to consciously or unconsciously shape your thoughts, feelings and behaviors as you interacted with them.

Did you know that when we're in close friendship or a romantic relationship with someone that we're also participating in a social system? That's right; two people can be their very own social system. And like all social systems, a friendship or a romantic relationship serves a function. These types of relationships can provide a source of social support to help with our physical or financial needs; they can provide answers to questions we may have; and can even provide us with a sense of emotional support by increasing our sense of belonging and boosting our self-esteem. And like all social systems, there's social influence going on. That means that in a close friendship or romantic relationship, just like in family relationships, direct and indirect conditioning shapes the thoughts, attitudes and behaviors of the two people within the relationship.

Our Relationship with Fear
(Emotional Convergence)

As you learned in Chapter Two, the years of childhood conditioning that we received in our family social system has had a profound effect on the development and maintenance of our fears. But we can be conditioned by our current close relationships (e.g., husband or wife, boyfriend or girlfriend, best friend, roommate, etc.) as well. And these relationships don't take years to exert their influence over us; it can happen in a matter of days, weeks or months.

Research shows that roommates and dating couples who've been in relationships for as little as 6 months often find that their emotions have become similar over time. This is known as *emotional convergence.* This emotional similarity between the two people in a relationship helps to keep them together because it reduces the chance that they'll have conflicting opinions or have different approaches to solving life's problems. Similarity in attitudes and behaviors helps to keep the two people bonded to each other and also helps to keep their relationship stable.

That similarity also makes it easier for them to coordinate their thoughts and actions — they're essentially "on the same page" in terms of their thoughts, feelings and behavioral responses. What's even more interesting is that the partner with less power in the relationship changes over time to become more like the other person. This also increases the stability of the relationship and keeps the two people emotionally connected.

Studies show that dating couples who stay together are emotionally similar to each other and the couples who break up are less emotionally similar to each other. In fact, the couples that stay together find that their relationship becomes stronger and they become even more alike in their values and attitudes. Even their social skills, mental abilities and behaviors get more similar to each other compared to when they first started dating. This is adaptive because, in response to any external threat, the two people can coordinate their thoughts and behaviors to help them jointly deal with the threat. Because they both think similar things and want to act in similar ways, it gets faster and easier for them to coordinate a joint response. As such, emotional convergence is a very powerful phenomenon.

My husband and I have emotionally converged, and I hadn't realized how much until recently. Although we shared many similarities while we were dating (same values, sense of humour, attitude toward physical fitness, loyalty to family and friends, etc.) and had a very cohesive relationship, we weren't aware of how much more we'd grown to be alike until after we married and moved in together. At first I noticed that I was adopting some of his speech patterns and that he was adopting some of mine. Soon we began to finish each other's' sentences, simultaneously blurt out the same comments in response to a particular situation, or come to the exact same conclusion about an issue we were considering. When this first happened we'd look at each other in amazement and say "I was just going to say that" or "I was thinking the exact same thing."

About a year ago, something happened that drove the point home even further. We wanted to take some time off work because we'd both had a busy year and needed some down time. Since I'd never been to Las Vegas and he'd been there several times with his friends before we met, we made a decision that we'd spend our vacation there. I was excited to see one of the famous Vegas shows, do some shopping, and take day trips to the Grand Canyon and Hoover Dam. He was excited to show me his favourite spots along the strip and to take me on a motorcycle ride in the desert as he'd done with a friend some years before. So, we went to the travel agent to begin making arrangements and excitedly looked forward to our upcoming Vegas trip in a month's time.

A few days after visiting the travel agent I found myself sitting at my office desk and thinking that perhaps a Vegas trip wasn't the best option for our vacation at that point in time. After all, I had had an extremely busy year, had many deadlines and seminars ahead of me, and a growing list of clients to see when I returned. So I made the decision that I'd let him know that I'd changed my mind about Vegas and hope that he wouldn't be too disappointed when I asked to postpone this trip until the following year.

To my surprise, during our usual lunch time phone call, before I got the chance to tell him about my change of heart, he told me that he'd had a change of heart about us going to Las Vegas. Instead, he thought that a more relaxed beach vacation would be better for us. We'd come to the same new decision about where to spend our vacation! Although I'd made my decision independently from my husband, and he from mine, our emotional convergence had led us to the same conclusion at the same time. Emotional convergence was once again demonstrated by our similar patterns of thinking about a situation and had further strengthened our already cohesive relationship.

So what does emotional convergence have to do with our fears? Everything! I believe that *when we habitually have fear responses to stressors, we are by default having a long term relationship with our fear.* That's right. Just like we'd be in a relationship with a real person, I maintain that we'd be in a relationship with a personification named "Fear"; just like if Fear was a real person in our lives.

That means that like in any long term relationship, through emotional convergence and social influence, when we enter into a relationship with Fear we also end up adopting some of his characteristics (just like we adopt the characteristics of another person in our relationships with other human being). And in this relationship Fear is the more powerful one. So, over time, we end up adjusting our thoughts, feelings and behaviors to be more like Fear — we adopt his emotional and behavioral response to the stressors in our life.

FEAR FACT #12: When you habitually respond with fear to stressors, it's like you're in a long-term relationship with a person named Fear. And just like you're conditioned by your human relationships, you're also conditioned by Fear.

I use this analogy with my clients to let them see how, like any human social system, a personal relationship can either be healthy/functional or unhealthy/dysfunctional. Unfortunately, an ongoing dependent relationship with Fear is always unhealthy and dysfunctional. It leaves us little or no room for self-expression and limits our emotional and mental growth. Moreover, this relationship is emotionally draining and prevents us from moving forward and on to a more self-directed and successful life. Our ongoing dysfunctional relationship with Fear means that we have a breakdown in one or more of our internal systems. And, as with any breakdown, it will need to be addressed in order for the overall system to function effectively.

When Our Relationship with Fear becomes Dysfunctional

A typical causal sequence in a dysfunctional relationship is that it gradually progresses from an early "honeymoon" phase where both partner's needs are initially met to a later "imbalanced" phase where one partner's needs always takes priority over the other's. In the later stages of a dysfunctional relationship, there's always a giver and a taker, and the relationship becomes mentally, emotionally and/or physically harmful to one or both of the people involved. The progression is usually so incremental that the deterioration of the relationship doesn't even register in our conscious awareness until it has already started to cause us harm.

When you first met Fear, for example, he showed you only his good side; his supportive side. When you first entered into a relationship with Fear, you may have found that some of your needs were indeed met; a sign of a positive and healthy relationship. After all, didn't Fear activate your fight-or-flight response so that on a particular evening you didn't take that short-cut down the alleyway that you've always taken to get home because he alerted you that this time it would be dangerous to do so? Didn't Fear help you to avoid some rather emotionally stressful situations like getting you out of making that speech at your friend's wedding, or keep you from asking your boss for that raise that she'd promised you at your last performance review? Back in the honeymoon phase of the relationship, Fear really seemed to have your interests at heart.

But soon after you became emotionally invested in the relationship (after Fear got into your system), you discovered that he had a dark side as well. In fact, the longer you stayed with him the more of his dark side you saw. Over time you noticed that Fear had changed; he was more demanding of your time and energy. He was jealous if you didn't pay attention to him all the time and insisted on having input into all your decision-making. As the days, weeks, months and perhaps even years went by, you noticed that Fear was calling most of the shots in your life and that somewhere along the line, the other parts of you seemed to have faded into the background — you now thought, felt and behaved the way Fear wanted you to think, feel and behave. What happened? How did you become so powerless and Fear become so powerful?

What happened was that your ongoing relationship with Fear had become dysfunctional. You now both relate to each other in co-dependent and unhealthy ways. Fear became controlling and domineering and you've become fearful and anxious that you can't live without him even though you're failing to thrive in the relationship. Your needs are no longer met which is a sign of an unhealthy relationship. As is usual for an unhealthy or dysfunctional relationship, issues of control and power have taken centre stage.

In your relationship with Fear, you're out of control and powerless in terms of your dependence on him, and he's out of control in terms of his insistence on having and maintaining power over you. Your own personal boundaries about what you're willing to put up with in the relationship have been eroded by Fear's manipulation of your sense of self — he now controls what you think, feel and do. He becomes the barrier between you and your dreams and goals for your life.

But like many people, you weren't aware of just how dysfunctional the relationship was until it was too late. It isn't your fault that you didn't see it coming because the relationship didn't start out unhealthy, but rather, it slowly deteriorated over time. However, a dysfunctional relationship always has warning signs.

Some of the signs of a dysfunctional relationship include feeling:

- Powerless
- Frustrated
- Tense
- Uncertain
- Insecure
- Trapped
- Manipulated
- Unhappy
- Unworthy
- Dissatisfied
- Unfulfilled

Because our relationship with Fear is dysfunctional, it causes us more harm than good. It harms us mentally, emotionally and physically, and therefore has considerable consequences for our internal systems. *At the core of our dysfunctional relationship with Fear is a dysfunctional relationship with ourselves; with our own brain, mind, body and spirit.* This internal dysfunctional relationship was due, in large part, to our early conditioning and has been reinforced by the conditioning we continue to receive from our external social systems and our ongoing self-conditioning of our internal systems. In fact, the ongoing self-conditioning that happens when we continually give into our fearFULL thoughts, feelings and actions is the best way that Fear keeps his hold on us. At a certain point he doesn't even need input from our external environment anymore; our internal systems have been set on automatic and respond with fear to emotional stressors as a result of habit. In this way, Fear creates ongoing dysfunction in our internal operating systems.

Fear and Our Systems

We use and benefit from internal operating systems all the time, perhaps without even knowing that we're doing so. Our internal systems consist of physiological systems (like our cardiovascular system, our circulatory system, our reproductive system, and our digestive system) and eight other systems in our body. We've seen in Chapter Two how being under chronic stress (like when someone is continually fearful) can impact our cardiovascular system and our digestive system. But we're much more than just a collection of human physiological and biological body systems.

We also have brain and mind systems that interact with our body systems and influence our perceptions about whether something is a stressor or not. It's this interaction among our internal systems that can help or hinder our ability to confront and overcome our fears — they can work for us or against us.

Fear uses our internal systems against us by affecting what we think (brain), how we feel (mind) and what we do (body).

Our internal and external systems constantly interact with each other and provide feedback to each other. For example how we think (internal) affects our behavior and how we behave effects how others (external) react to us. When we get feedback from how others respond to us, this information in turn further influences the way we think, feel and behave. Our fears then are based on our internal mental, emotional and behavioral responses to the external cues we get from our environment.

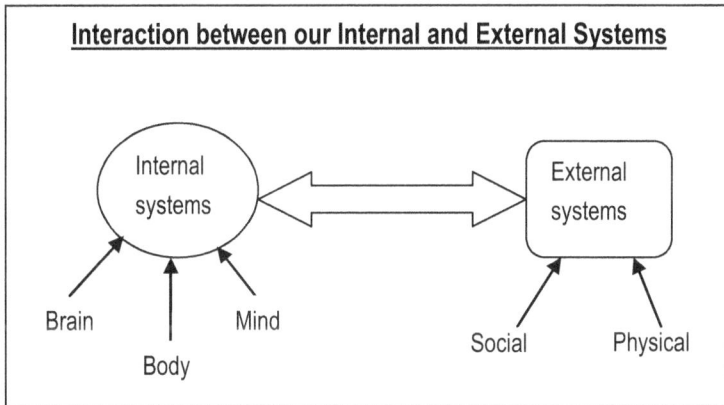

Interaction between our Internal and External Systems

Let's take Joan as an example. Joan has a fear of social rejection that stems from her time in elementary school where she was ridiculed by other students about her crooked teeth. Even after she got braces and her teeth became straight, Joan still bears the emotional scars left by years of teasing and rejection. Although time passed and Joan finished college and started a career, her fear of being rejected never left her. She still saw herself as the little girl with the crooked teeth that others had made fun of. This self-perception has affected her self-esteem and it's difficult for her to make new friends at her new job.

Because of her fear of being rejected, Joan tends to isolate herself from her colleagues and hesitates to accept invitations to socialize at lunch or after work. But the more she withdraws from other people, they in turn, no longer ask her to join them in their social activities because they've learned that she will turn down the invitation. This reinforces Joan's insecurity and fear that people don't like her and she feels even more rejected. Joan's fear of being socially rejected has become a *self-fulfilling prophesy* (i.e., a prediction that causes itself to become a reality).

Was Joan doomed to live a life filled with fear of being rejected? Of course not. At any time Joan could have made a conscious decision to overcome her fear barrier and take steps to change the way she thinks, feel and acts. She could begin to confront her prior childhood conditioning and take control over the way her dysfunctional relationship with Fear has impacted her present life and would continue to cast a shadow over her future. Rather than turning down opportunities to socialize with her colleagues, Joan could take advantage of these opportunities to help her reprogram her internal systems to think, feel and act like she was a well-liked and valuable member of the team. This new change in her attitude and behavior would then influence Joan's colleagues in terms of their perception of her and they would come to see her in a new light.

As we can see from this example, the mutually-reinforcing relationship between our internal and external systems is an extremely important one. This relationship can either work to help us overcome and eliminate our fear, or can work to continue to reinforce and keep us in a dysfunctional relationship with our fear. It's important to remember that although we may have initially been conditioned for fear by our external systems (particularly our social environment and early childhood conditioning), the starting point to overcoming our fears always lie within us — within our internal systems.

FEAR FACT #13: Your internal and external systems work together to either reinforce your fears or help you to confront and overcome your fears.

Emotions are the way we relate to our external systems and Fear distorts that relationship. When you're in an ongoing dysfunctional relationship with Fear, your internal systems (i.e., brain, mind, body and spirit) become wired to see life from Fear's point of view. Just like in human dysfunctional relationships where the more powerful person sets the tone for the relationship through emotional convergence, Fear will set the tone for your relationship with him. He'll manipulate you and eventually take control of your internal systems which will, in turn, have an impact on how you perceive and interact with your external systems (i.e., your physical and social environment) which will then influence how your external systems relate to you. It's a cycle that feeds on itself.

FEAR FACT #14: Your ongoing relationship with Fear affects your mental, physical and emotional systems.

As I teach about in my *Get Wired2Succeed* programs, the relationship between our internal and external systems play an important role in how we see ourselves and our ability to control our own destiny. The problem is, many of the systems that most people are using are flawed and operate below their level of conscious awareness. Most people have flawed internal operating systems and also have a flawed perception of their external systems. As such, their personal and professional life fails to function successfully and they keep spinning their wheels; unable to get out of their own way.

Remember, by definition, all systems need each of their component parts to work perfectly together in order for the entire system to function at its best. Remaining in a dysfunctional relationship with Fear has real consequences for our brain, mind and body systems because this relationship affects us mentally, emotionally and physically. This is because of the interconnectedness between these three internal systems. Whenever we stay in a dysfunctional relationship with Fear, we give up real long-term emotional security for the short-term false sense of emotional security that he provides.

In order for you to get your internal systems working together and functioning in perfect harmony, you'll need to understand how Fear is influencing your brain, mind and body systems. You'll need to know this in order to get Fear "out of your system." The next three chapters examine each of these three systems in detail and describe how they're affected by our relationship with Fear.

Chapter Four
Fear and Our Brain Systems

"A cat bitten once by a snake dreads even rope."
Arab Proverb

"Brain: an apparatus with which we think we think."
Ambrose Bierce

When we're in an ongoing relationship with Fear, he takes up residence in our brain. From there he can control many of our thoughts, emotions and behavioral responses. Our brain is the control center of our central nervous system. Our central nervous system consists of our brain, our spinal cord and peripheral nerves. Together, they coordinate all the activities in our body. Our brain is responsible for things like coordinating our actions, processing the information we take in from our environment, and also plays a role in our memory and emotions.

Our brain is an amazing muscle containing more than 100 billion nerve cells (call neurons) which are each interconnected by neural networks. These neural networks are made up of groups of functionally associated neurons (i.e., nerve cells that perform similar biological or chemical functions). Neurons are responsible for transmitting electrochemical signals from and to our brain — they're like a highway where our electrochemical signals can travel back and forth. When we keep repeating the same things over time (like when we develop a habit of thinking, feeling or behaving in certain ways) the connections between these neurons in our brain become stronger — our highway gets an express lane.

The brain is something physical; we can see the brain in various medical imaging techniques such as x-rays, fMRI (functional magnetic resonance imaging), and CT scans (computerized axial tomography). Scans such as the fMRI measure brain activity and neural activity. They can show, for example, which areas of our brain are activated when we respond to certain stressors. This ability to see how specific areas of our brain behave as we interact with our physical or emotional environment is used in brain mapping.

Our brain plays a crucial role in our body's perception of and response to things and situations that cause us to feel fear. There are cells and regions in our brain that constantly transfer and respond to information coming from our internal and external systems. However, certain parts of our brain play a more central role in our fear response than others.

Brain mapping has shown that fear has a real physical home in our brain. The part of our brain where fear is located is called the *amygdala*. It's known as the "fear center" and is a very primitive part of our brain. It's most active when we feel fearful, anxious or threatened. The amygdala is shaped a bit like an almond and is located deep within our temporal lobe. We have two temporal lobes (one on either side of our head just by our ears) and so we have two amygdalae. Our temporal lobes are responsible for processing and organizing sensory input from our environment, as well as our speech and language comprehension.

The *hippocampus* is also located in our temporal lobe and is the part of our brain that puts together all the bits of information we take in and puts them into our short-term and long-term memory (just like we have two amygdalae we also have two hippocampi). People who suffer from Alzheimer's disease, for example, have damage to their hippocampus which is why they have memory loss and often get disoriented. Our hippocampus works with our amygdala to integrate any new information or experience with existing information we already have in our memory to make the new information or new experience meaningful for us.

Our *prefrontal cortex* is located in the front part of our brain (just behind our forehead above our eyes) and is responsible for higher level thinking and decision-making. It's a more evolved part of our brain and is the last area of the brain to mature (generally by the time we're 25 years-old). It's where we make social judgments; weigh various alternatives before making a decision; anticipate the consequences of our behavior; and where we plan our behavior so that we can move towards a specific goal that we've set for ourselves.

These three parts of our brain are very important to Fear. He uses them to control our ability to perceive things clearly and to think logically. He knows very well that we use our brain to help us interpret whether the things, people and situations in our life are a source of threat or not and to make appropriate decisions about what action to take. However, when Fear takes up residence in our brain, more likely than not, he'll make a habit of directing our brain to tell us that "yes" the source is indeed a threat and activate a fight-or-flight response. He'll do this for physical threats as well as potential emotional threats.

Moreover, he won't always direct us to take actions that are in our own best interest — in fact, he's very likely to tell us to do something that runs against our own best interest. He'll manipulate and pressure us to surrender our own personal power and give him control over our life. He does this, in part, by controlling our brain because he knows that what happens there significantly impacts the way we think and feel, as well as the choices we make.

Fear prevents Us from Thinking Rationally

When we're in fight-or-flight mode our brain prepares us *psychologically* for action by increasing activity in our amygdala and hippocampus and suppressing activity in our prefrontal cortex. That's because, when we're in fight-or-flight mode our brain is focused entirely on just two options; stay and fight or run away (although sometimes "freezing" on the spot can occur if we become overwhelmed with panic and have a "deer in the headlights" response to the threat). But whatever action we take, we do something. Our brain doesn't want us to waste valuable time thinking and processing a bunch of options because that might keep us in a dangerous situation. For example, when you're experiencing fear from a physical or environmental stressor, your brain doesn't say: "you should just stay here and think about possible responses before you calmly decide what to do and then proceed in an orderly manner". No, instead your brain sends the urgent message "Get out fast!" or "Fight back now!" That's it.

When we feel threatened and our brain goes into fight-or-flight mode, the activity in our amygdala takes over and the activity in our pre-frontal cortex is told to take a back seat. This has been referred to as the *amygdala hijack*. Our primitive amygdala knows that the time it takes for us to respond to a physical or environmental threat could mean the difference between life and death (such as when someone is trying to avoid colliding with the car in front of them). So, the amygdala makes sure that the time between when we sense a threat and when we respond to the threat can occur within a few thousandths of a second.

That's why we often can't think rationally in fight-or-flight mode and can often jump to the wrong conclusions by misinterpreting the strength of the stressor (i.e., thinking that things are far worse than they actually are). It's because our amygdala has "hijacked" our brain and is doing the thinking for us, not our prefrontal cortex. What matters to our brain at that moment is surviving, and things like intellectual tasks aren't even being considered.

FEAR FACT #15: Fear can cause you to think irrationally because the part of your brain responsible for logical thinking has been switched off when you're experiencing a fear response.

Again, this works well and was adaptive when we were on the run from hungry predators and other physical threats. However, it's not as adaptive in today's world when we have to deal with emotional or psychological stressors, like trying to stay calm during an important work presentation or not saying something that you might later regret during an argument with a friend, or your husband or wife.

Emotional stressors or threats cause the *exact same* fear response (fight-or-flight) that physical stressors do. For example, when someone feels "attacked" by someone in a verbal argument, their fight-or-flight reaction kicks into high gear just as much as if they were being physically attacked. But the fact that they can't think logically and rationally when they're in fight-or-flight mode means that they can't focus on the proper solutions to their emotional problems when they're experiencing fear. As such, they might "fight" by continuing to argue even when the other person stops arguing or even combine their verbal counterattacks with actual physical threats if they feel cornered. Or, they might want to "flee" from the verbal attack by walking away from the other person or emotionally withdrawing from them during the argument. Just like if they were in a real physical confrontation, their automatic fight-or-flight says "it's them or me" and they fight or try to get out of the situation.

The same thing happens when we're being controlled by Fear — we can't think of rational solutions to the challenges facing us because our challenges are keeping us in a state of fear, and when we're experiencing fear we can't see the solutions. It's a catch 22 where the only options we see are to fight or to flee. This fear-based tunnel vision, is shown by research, to limit our ability to make proper judgments, to learn and remember, and even affects our ability to make good decisions and solve problems.

Let's take Paul as an example. Paul and his wife have been divorced for three years and they share joint custody of their two children: a 7 year-old boy and a 10-year old girl. The children stay with Paul on the weekends and at times during the week because Paul and his ex-wife have a flexible custody arrangement. However, recently Paul's ex-wife has become engaged and Paul isn't dealing with it too well. In fact, Paul is full of fear.

He's afraid that this new man in his children's life will eventually take over as their father figure and push him to the side. Paul has become increasingly agitated whenever he drops the children off at their mother's house and has begun to be more permissive with them. For example, he's gone against the rules that he and his ex-wife had previously set for the children and is allowing them to stay up past their bedtimes on school nights, lets them eat junk food for all their meals, and watch television shows that aren't age appropriate. He feels a new need to have his children like him at all costs and is reluctant to scold them or set boundaries for fear that they won't want to spend time with him anymore. As a result of his lax parenting, his children have become more demanding and defiant not only with Paul, but also with their mother. Their grades have been slipping and his son's teacher has complained about his disruptive behavior in class.

The more Paul's ex-wife tries to talk with him about the situation, the more Paul takes offence and accuses her of trying to poison the children's mind against him. Paul's ex-wife is growing increasingly frustrated with her inability to communicate with Paul and is considering going to court to address the issue by seeking sole custody of their two children. The situation has spiraled out of control and Paul can't seem to keep his fearful emotions in check. To his thinking, he's in a desperate battle to keep his children from growing attached to another potential father figure and he's oblivious to the fact that his actions are putting his relationship with his children at risk. He's blind to the fact that he, not his ex-wife or her fiancé, is threatening his relationship with his children.

Paul has let his relationship with Fear control his response to the perceived threat of his ex-wife's upcoming marriage. He's let Fear cloud his normally rational brain from thinking about a win-win solution to the issue of how best to integrate his ex-wife's fiancé into their children's lives. His judgment has been compromised by being in fight mode (due to fight-or-flight arousal in his amygdala and the suppression of his prefrontal cortex) and the once peaceful and cooperative joint custody arrangement he's had with his wife is now threatened. He stands to lose the very thing (his children) that he fears losing.

Like Paul, whenever Fear takes hold of your brain, he makes sure that you operate in fight-or-flight mode most of the time. That way he can bypass your rational, thinking brain where you weigh alternatives, do your planning and arrive at logical solutions to your problems. From his vantage point in your brain, Fear can then manipulate you and keep you in a state where your thinking is distorted and you're likely to see threats where none exists and you overreact to even the smallest fear-trigger . When Fear has you in this state, he directs your focus to short-term survival — all you can think about is the situation directly in front of you and you act without thinking about the potential long-term consequences of your decisions. For example, let's say that you're in a group meeting with your boss and she asks you to give an update of your team's project at work. However, the very thought of that fills you with fear even though you know everyone in the room and every single detail of the project. So you pass on the opportunity and someone else gives the presentation and gets the attention and eventually the promotion that you've been hoping for. The short-term benefit of avoiding making the presentation is nothing compared to the long-term benefit of what would have happened financially, professionally and emotionally if you'd just faced your fear and given the presentation.

Some questions you might want to ask yourself at this point include:

1. How has fear caused me to act irrationally in the past or recently? How has my focus on short-term gain prevented me from getting even better long-term benefits?
2. What was I thinking during the time the situation was happening?
3. What was I feeling (emotionally and physically) during the time the situation was happening?
4. Looking back, how did I feel about the way I handled the situation?
5. Looking back, how did others feel about the way I handled the situation?
6. Do I have a pattern of reacting without thinking when I feel fearful?

7. What other options could I have tried to handle the situation?
8. What could have been a win-win solution to the situation?
9. If I'm currently reacting irrationally with fear to a situation or to someone, how can I change things to arrive at a win-win solution?
10. How would my life be better if I made the choice to think, feel and act differently about this situation or person?

These questions will help you to determine if the thing or situation you're thinking about that's causing you to have a fear response is a rational or irrational reaction. They'll help you to see if you have a habitual way of responding when you experience fear, and to see that there are other options available for you to escape this patterned response. When you do this exercise you take away Fear's power to control your thoughts and emotions and will help you move beyond habitual irrational behavioral reactions to stressors. This is yet another step towards breaking down your fear barriers.

Fear Messes with Our Memory

Part of Fear's manipulation of our brain involves him playing games with our memory. Fear doesn't want us to think rationally and will even stop us from remembering things that might help us solve the problem or situation that's causing us to feel fearful. He wants to keep us feeling afraid and does this by using our fight-or-flight response against us.

As you now know, during a fear-response, our amygdala hijacks our brain, diverts blood away from our prefrontal cortex and causes stress hormones to course though our body. This significantly limits our ability to focus and effectively problem solve. Research using animal and human subjects show that stress hormones influence the memory process. It's even been speculated that diverting blood and oxygen from the prefrontal cortex to the amygdala during a fight-or-flight response is like temporarily losing 10-15 IQ points.

FEAR FACT #16: Fear can cause you to temporarily forget familiar people and places, recent events, and even some of the personal details of your own life.

It's been scientifically proven that we actually become less intelligent when we're operating in a state of fear. Essentially, we're thinking with less capacity and brain power when we're under stress and experiencing fear due to the over-secretion of stress hormones. This impacts our ability to think and recall things that we can easily remember when we're not under stress. In essence, *Fear makes our brain go blank at a time when we need it the most.* When we're experiencing a fear-response to a stressor, it takes us longer to remember things that were recently learned and it also takes us longer to remember the things that we learned some time ago.

I have my own personal experience of having my amygdala hijacked because of fear. It happened to me during the early stages of my divorce. As you may recall from the Preface, I chose to end my marriage while I was still a graduate student because the relationship has grown dysfunctional and was affecting my mental and physical health. The marriage had become a source of chronic stress for me and, combined with the requirements of the doctoral program, lecturing several times a week, studying for my comprehensive exams, conducting research and writing my dissertation, I was under a great deal of stress. Divorce is ranked second in terms of stressful life events (right after the death of a spouse) and I did experience stress as a result of terminating a relationship with someone I'd known since I was in my early 20's. However, the divorce was also a source of stress-relief because it removed me from a stressful living situation, gave me an opportunity for introspection, and allowed me to regain the power I'd slowly given up over the course of the relationship.

However, like all divorces, other things came into play after the decision was made. One of the most stressful parts of the process for me was dealing with the financial consequences of going from a two-person to a one-person household income. In addition to the financial stress of having to pay 100% of the bills with only 50% of the household income, I was simultaneously coping with academic stress, family and friend stress (as they adjusted to the news of the divorce) and the additional financial stress of paying lawyer's fees on a graduate student's salary. Nothing caused me to feel stress and fear more than those visits to my lawyer's office. It seemed that almost everything he did came with a surprisingly hefty bill.

My first visit to his office was in the middle of the day on my lunch break. I was lecturing later that afternoon and was anxious to hear about the divorce process and its associated costs before I had to get back to the campus. The appointment went by in a blur of emotion combined with my attempts to understand the legalities associated with dissolving a marriage. A few weeks and several legal bills later, I had another appointment with the lawyer. I was running late so decided to take a taxi rather than take the time to go home to retrieve my car.

As I got into the taxi I scolded myself for not having left the campus earlier because I was now on a strict budget and taxi rides were a luxury that I couldn't afford. I gave the taxi driver the name of the intersection he should drive towards and settled down for the ride. But as I sat in the back of the car I started thinking about the mounting legal bills and the fact that I was going to quickly run out of money if the process dragged on much longer. Although I was under considerable chronic stress, the one thing that was causing me to experience fear was the cost of the divorce itself and the financial struggle of remaining in graduate school until I finished writing my dissertation. Suddenly, in the middle of my thoughts, my heart started beating irregularly and my brain felt like it had stopped working.

I'd been in the taxi for just a few minutes and had given the driver the instructions to head north. But now I was suddenly unsure. Was the lawyer's office north or south of where we were? I had no idea. I hadn't taken his business card and I didn't have a cell phone with me. I couldn't remember my lawyer's name, the firm's name, or where it was located in the city. I looked outside the windows of the taxi and the familiar city that I knew seemed to have disappeared from view. I became confused about my surroundings and panicked. I knew the city I was in, but all the buildings looked unfamiliar. It was as if I hadn't seen them before; like I was in a foreign city instead of the city I'd been in for 10 years.

Feeling unsure of myself, I told the driver to stop and turn the taxi around and said that I'd given him the wrong directions. The sense of panic that I felt because of my disorientation was compounded with the fear that I knew that I'd be billed for the entire appointment even if I was late. The driver looked puzzled, but turned the taxi around and began to drive south. As we drove south, I second-guessed myself again because I felt that we were still going in the wrong direction. I felt completely lost and confused. What was happening to me? Why couldn't I think clearly? I recalled my research on dementia and my interaction with Alzheimer's patients and empathized that this must be how it felt to be demented — to have a memory loss that affects one's ability to make decisions and find oneself in an environment that should be familiar but suddenly seems strange and foreboding.

Thankfully, after a few deep breaths to slow down my heart rate and positive visualizations to focus my attention, I was able to bring my cognitive functioning back to its normal state. I prompted my prefrontal cortex back into action and freed myself from the tyranny of my amygdala. With each deep breath, oxygenated blood was redirected from my amygdala back to my prefrontal cortex allowing me to focus on solving the problem of remembering the location of my lawyer's office. It was for me, a first-hand experience of what stress and strong emotion (fear in my case) can do to one's memory. Although I initially worried about the long-term effects of that frightening experience, my memory immediately went back to what it had been before I was exposed to Fear's temporary hijack of my brain.

I'd read research studies that showed that people experiencing prolonged stress can find it difficult to recall recent events, familiar people and even forget some of the personal details of their own life. But having experienced it personally gave me a whole new respect for the effects of fear and stress on cognitive functioning, particularly short-term memory loss. I relate this experience to clients who are finding that they have become increasingly forgetful due to the stress of divorce, employment, marital or family problems and the fear that they won't be able to cope with what life is presenting to them. I let them know that these symptoms are simply the result of the "amygdala hijack" and teach them techniques to overcome the additional fear that comes with this experience.

Has your mind ever gone blank while you were experiencing a fear response? Did you forget even simple things that caused you to feel anxious and upset which made your fear response even worse than it was originally? If so, now you know that this was a normal response to experiencing high levels of stress and fear. When you learn to control your dysfunctional relationship with Fear, you'll be able control the amygdala hijack of your brain.

Fear Fools Us into Believing What's False is True

It's also important to know that *our brain can be easily fooled.* That's because our brain doesn't distinguish between what's real and what's just based on our perception or what we're imagining. This is another way that Fear uses the way our brain functions against us in order to keep us under his control. If he can control us not just with things that are actually happening, but also with things that might happen or aren't really happening at all, then he can control not only our present, but also our future.

How does Fear do this? Let's take an example of what happens to our brain when we watch certain types of movies. Let's say that you've gone to the movies with your best friend, have bought your large popcorn and drink, and are sitting comfortably in your seat. You're relaxed and joking with your friend as you both discuss the thriller you're about to see and where you'll go for dinner afterwards. Then the lights go out, the surround-sound speakers blast sound and vibration into the theatre, and the movie appears on the large screen in front of you. As the movie progresses you get caught up in the story; it holds your attention. Your hand becomes still in your container of popcorn as your eyes and ears fixate on what's happening on the screen. As you watch, a menacing masked figure with a chainsaw approaches a cabin full of unsuspecting vacationing teenagers and turns the knob on the cabin door. You're not aware of it, but your pupils have dilated, your stomach is clenched, your breathing has become rapid and your muscles have tightened in anticipation of what will follow. You're experiencing fear!

But why in the world are you afraid? The movie isn't real. It's just a bunch of pixels projected on a 2-dimensional piece of fabric hung from the theatre ceiling. In reality you're sitting comfortably in your seat beside your best friend, with your hand in a container of buttery popcorn, surrounded by hundreds of other people (who are all also experiencing fear). You're perfectly safe but your brain perceives that you're in danger as you identify with the characters on the screen.

You're experiencing fear because as you watch the movie, your brain has been watching the movie too. It senses a threat (the masked figure with the chainsaw) and has sent out fight-or-flight signals to your body which is now activated to deal with the threat (to fight or to run away). Your amygdala doesn't know that the movie isn't real; all it knows is what it perceives. Because it perceives a threat, it has turned down the activity in your prefrontal cortex just like it would if the situation was really happening. You aren't thinking rationally at this moment, all you're doing is feeling, and you're feeling fear even when there's no real threat to you.

This is one of the ways that Fear controls us. When we're in a relationship with Fear, he not only wants to control what's happening in reality, he wants to control what's happening in our imagination. He fools our brain to feel fear in situations in when no real threat exists. Research using diagnostic imaging technologies such as fMRI (functional magnetic resonance imaging) scans show, for example, that the same parts of the brain get activated regardless of whether we're doing a task in real life, or just imaging it in our head. So when we're experiencing fear, either because we're faced with a stressor right in front of us, or imagining what "might" happen in the future, Fear makes sure that our brain is set on fight-or-flight arousal.

FEAR FACT #17: Fear lies to you by making you believe that the things you fear in your imagination are actually real.

If you're faced with a real threat in front of you, especially a physical threat, then fight-or-flight arousal may be a good and functional way to deal with the situation. However, having a fear-response to an imagined threat that may or may not even happen at some point in the future serves no functional purpose whatsoever. It's actually helps to keep you in fear by reinforcing your fear response. You're activating your fight-or-flight arousal system and experiencing fear symptoms unnecessarily simply by thinking about what might happen. Again, Fear does this to control your perception, not only about the present, but about what the future might hold for you. He doesn't want you to think that you'll be able to handle the situations that might come your way; he wants to keep you insecure and uncertain about your own personal power.

Some questions you might want to ask yourself when you're experiencing a fear response are:

1. Am I reacting to something that is real (is actually happening) or something that I'm only thinking about (may or may not happen in the future)?
2. If it's not happening now, what evidence (real, factual and rational) do I have to show that this may actually happen in the future?
3. Because the event actually hasn't happened yet, how realistic is my current fear response?

4. Does my current thinking and feelings about what might happen in the future move me any further towards finding a solution to the problem?

5. How is thinking about what might happen in the future contributing to my current fear response and making matters worse?

6. If I imagine a worst case scenario, where the very thing I'm imagining actually happens, how could I use it as a learning experience and actually grow emotionally or mentally from the experience?

7. What specific steps can I take now to make sure that what I'm imagining doesn't actually happen (note that this doesn't include you trying to avoid the stressor in any way)?

8. How do I feel when I imagine a best case scenario; a scenario where I'm able to cope appropriately with the stressor and confront my fear?

9. What parts of my best case scenario can I focus on and work towards achieving right now?

10. What's the first step I can take; the second, the third, etc. towards helping to make my best case scenario come true?

These questions will help you to determine if your fear is real or just something that you're thinking about; something that might well not even happen. They will also help you to think about and feel what it would be like to be in a position where you have the confidence to confront and overcome your fear. It will also give you a hint as to how it might feel like to be on the other side of your fear. When you do this exercise you take away Fear's power to control your imagination and by default, your thoughts, emotions and actions. With each question you answer, you're breaking down Fear's hold over you.

Fear Makes Us do Foolish Things

When our amygdala is hijacked by Fear, we can do some foolish things because we're not thinking logically. Because our sympathetic nervous system is focused on a perceived threat and not on rational, reasoned thinking, we end up doing things that we would never do if we were thinking clearly. Many of my clients tell me about situations where they were clearly not themselves when they were operating under the control of Fear. Some have quit jobs without adequate financial planning after experiencing what they considered to be the final insult (e.g., mistreatment from a boss or getting passed over for a promotion); some have entered into problematic relationships (e.g., like agreeing to date someone who they know, deep down isn't a good person but they're afraid to be alone); and one or two have even lent large sums of money to friends who they wanted to hold on to knowing in their gut that the money would never be returned.

In all the above examples, they let Fear dictate their responses to stressors and did things, which in retrospect, they see as foolish. That's because judgment and decision-making generally involves emotion. So, when we make decisions while experiencing a fear-response we're making decisions that aren't being properly vetted by our prefrontal cortex (i.e., the reasoned, rational part of our brain). Research has shown, for example, that increased activity in the amygdala (and reducing the activity in the prefrontal cortex) affects people's judgment about the trustworthiness of others and influences their strategies about the types of gambles they're willing to take.

Unfortunately, I know all too well how Fear can cloud one's brain into making potentially life-changing decisions that seem foolish in retrospect. Let's take an example of the situation I found myself in when faced with the thought of leaving my dysfunctional marriage. I knew for some time that I wasn't happy; in fact, even my dreams were telling me that something was wrong. But the fear of leaving the marriage left me in a state of chronic indecision. I didn't know whether it was better to stay or to go (the approach-avoidance conflict that I spoke about in the Preface). I was desperate for an answer and looked for signs everywhere about what to do.

Before I tell you what I did, here's a little back story. My ex-husband and I lived on the 10th floor of a large apartment complex in the heart of the city. We had a long balcony and, in the first spring we were there, I planted several flower boxes and hanging planters. To my surprise, a mated pair of house finches quickly took up residence in one of the hanging planters. We watched them bring back twigs and string for the nest and were delighted by the many chirps coming out of the planter as they raised their little finch family. It was worth the inconvenience of avoiding that part of the balcony and being dive-bombed and angrily chirped at by the father finch as I watered the planters each day. Eventually the young finches would learn how to fly and they and their parents would disappear from the balcony. This pattern repeated itself for several springs.

Fast forward to a few years later when, one late-summer day, I found myself at a crossroads about what to do about my marriage. I was intent on making a decision that very day because I'd grown emotionally exhausted with thoughts about what to do and it was impacting my ability to concentrate fully on my doctoral studies. I found myself looking outside to the balcony and came to the conclusion that it would be best to terminate the marriage. I felt simultaneously relief and sadness but also a sense of peace with my decision. But, just as I'd made the decision, to my surprise, one of the house finches, which had been gone from our balcony for weeks, appeared on the balcony railing and began to chirp and sing to its heart's content.

I was puzzled and my heart started to race. What was the finch doing on the balcony at this late stage in the summer? Why was it facing me, and singing away, even when it saw me staring at it from just the other side of the window? Was this a message from the universe? Was the finch trying to tell me something? Well, to my emotionally exhausted brain, what else could this be but the long awaited-for sign, right? I suddenly feared that the decision I'd made just moments earlier to leave the marriage was the wrong one. The finch, I decided, had come to tell me not to give up but to stay in the marriage. So I stayed. Talk about giving up my personal power — I let my impression of a house finch's message determine my fate for goodness sake. How much poorer could one's judgement be?

When I share this story with my clients or in workshops, I get stares of shock and disbelief (after the laughter subsides). They have a hard time reconciling this ridiculous, desperate decision and poor judgement with the successful, confident and rational woman they see in front of them. But I let them know that, like them, when I existed in a state of fear, my ability to make proper decisions about my life was seriously compromised. Although I was arguably an intelligent person, I too made foolish decisions and had poor judgement based on my relationship with Fear. His hold on me was the most powerful relationship in my life at that time. Because of that dysfunctional relationship, I didn't exercise my own personal power, but instead, freely gave up that power to Fear. No wonder I couldn't succeed despite my best efforts. I was a puppet and Fear was pulling the strings.

> **FEAR FACT #18**: Fear clouds your judgment and you often end up making foolish decisions that you later regret.

When we're faced with decisions, Fear often clouds our judgement by boosting the activity in our amygdala and limiting the activity in our prefrontal cortex. We can't think rationally and often look for signs, something or someone else to make our decisions for us because we fear making the wrong one. Because Fear had control of my emotions, I ended up staying in my marriage for another two painful years — I clung to the very thing that was threatening my emotional well-being.

I have a little motivational picture I like to share with my clients. It's a picture of a teeny little frog clinging to the inside top row of teeth of a very large alligator with its mouth agape. The caption reads: *fear makes us cling to the strangest things*. At varying points in my life, Fear made me cling to a marriage, a job, and even some friends that weren't good for my mental or physical health. Instinctively we all know to fight or flee from physical threats. But something in our brain goes a little haywire when it comes to emotional threats. We don't always see these threats for what they are because of Fear, and indeed even cling to these threats rather than fighting or running away. This is another way that Fear keeps his hold on us. Has being in a state of fear ever made you do something that, in retrospect, seem foolish?

Fear deposits Fearful Memories in Our Brain Bank

So, by now you're learned that Fear stops us from thinking rationally; makes our mind go blank when we need it the most; makes us believe that what's false is actually true; and makes us do foolish things. Those four things alone should be enough reason to demonstrate that your relationship with Fear is dysfunctional, controlling and gets in the way of your ability to succeed in life. But as the advertisers on television infomercials say: "But wait. There's more!" Fear doesn't stop there; he has many more tricks up his sleeve to keep us under his control. And again, he uses this by turning our brain against us.

Not only does our brain tone down our ability to think rationally when we feel fear, but when we have a fear-response to a threat or stressor; the stressful memory is stored in our hippocampus where it leaves a permanent physical imprint (as long term memory). Research has shown that when we learn things while feeling highly emotional (like when we're feeling fearful), this creates and even stronger reaction and a stronger association in our brain between the stressor and your memory of it.

FEAR FACT #19: Your fearful reaction to stressors is stored as permanent physical neurological changes in your brain.

It's as if our amygdala is saying to our hippocampus: "This particular memory is really important, so make it a priority among the other memories. Make it a memorable memory" This makes it easier for us to retrieve that negative memory the next time we encounter that stressor because we become hyper-vigilant (i.e., we get overly sensitive to detecting threats in our environment) and over-reactive because our brain is now primed to look out for that particular threat. It's like our hippocampus keeps our amygdala on standby so that we're always in a state of anticipatory fight-or-flight. This also makes it more difficult for us to get rid of this memory.

It's the fact that we remember our specific experience of how we felt whenever something or someone caused us to feel fearful that makes Fear so powerful in our lives. For example, did you ever notice how easy it is to recall negative, fearful things that happened to you much easier than it is to recall positive, hopeful things? Do you notice how easy it is to remember an insult but how much more difficult it is to remember all the compliments you've received throughout your life? Each time you recall negative things that made you feel fearful in the past, your hippocampus and amygdala actually work together to cause you to experience the feeling associated with that memory just as if you were experiencing the fear trigger all over again.

The ability to keep highly emotional and fearful memories in the forefront of all our other memories is adaptive for physical or environmental threats (after all, it's a good thing that we only have to learn once not to approach a snarling wild animal or walk into oncoming traffic). However, it's often counter-productive when we experience ongoing fears associated with emotional or psychological threats such as the ones discussed in Chapter Two.

Let's take a simple example of deposits and withdrawals, like when you do your banking. When you deposit money into your account, it gets stored by the bank. You can go back and withdraw that money whenever you want; it's yours and only you have access to your account. The more money you deposit, the more you'll be able to withdraw. You can't withdraw what you haven't deposited. When you made your first deposits and withdrawals it was probably a little difficult since you didn't know the procedure. You might have needed help to fill out the paper deposit and withdrawal slips or using the instant teller machine. But with practice, you can now make your financial deposits and withdrawals with ease.

The same thing happens in our brain when we learn things as we interact with the world around us. Each time we learn something, no matter how small or simple, we make a deposit into our brain's memory bank. When we deposit things into our memory bank, it gets stored there and leaves a permanent physical change in our brain (scientists refer to this as an *engram*).

The more information (especially negative emotional information like when we felt fear) that we deposit and store in our memory bank, the more we can withdraw. The more withdrawals we make from our memory bank (i.e., when we pull from that storage of information), the easier it is to retrieve that information each time. This phenomenon is often referred to as the *law of exercise*. Depending on how many fear memories we store, and how often we retrieve them, these memories can become their own source of internal chronic stress for us, and can cause us to feel fear even when the actual threat isn't present.

You may have noticed that banks have express lines for business clients. That is, those clients don't have to line up with the regular customers to get their banking needs met; they have a line devoted solely to their need to get into the bank, get their business done, and get out quickly so they can get back to work. Well, Fear has an express line too. He has an express line from our hippocampus (where memories are stored) to our amygdala (where our fear response resides). Fear uses this express line to make it easier for us to make your fear deposits and withdrawals. So, when we're presented with a stressor, we don't even have to think about how we should react; Fear makes sure that the express line always works in his favor.

Just like a banking business express line or an airline boarding express line where the business and first-class travelers get served before all the other passengers, Fear's express line makes sure that his needs get met first. Fear uses his express line to our brain to get to our thoughts, emotions and actions before we have a chance to think, feel, or do anything else besides think, feel and act fearfully. He uses the express line in the neural wiring of our brain (our neural network) to bypass the other emotions that might be better able to help us when faced with a stressor. Remember the express lane example I used on the first page of this Chapter? Well that's how Fear beats the other emotions to the finish line — when you're presented with a stressor, Fear takes the express lane while your other, more functional emotions are stuck in traffic.

> **FEAR FACT #20**: The more often you've reacted to stressors with fear in the past, the easier it will be for you to react with fear in the present and in the future.

Let's take another example. Have you ever been taking a leisurely walk through the park or walking trail and been startled by a twig or piece of rope that you've seen lying on the ground out of the corner of your eye? At soon as your brain made a note of this thing you froze and became fearful. This happened even before you were consciously aware that it was a rope or twig and not a snake. The fear that it might be a snake, and the resulting fight-or-flight response, came well before your conscious realization of what the thing on the ground really was. Your fear took the express line right to your amygdala and bypassed your prefrontal cortex. It was only a fraction of a second later, when you were able to really look at the thing on the ground and see with your prefrontal cortex, and not with your amygdala, that it was not a snake, that you were able to consciously control your stress response.

Storing negative memories or associations is how conditioning affects our brain (remember Fear Facts #6, #7 and #8). That's because each time we react with fear, we're building up the strength and number of neural connections in key areas of our brain just like if we were putting them in an express line.

Each time we're exposed to the stressor and react with the same fear response, these stimulus-response connections mesh together in our hippocampus (like a wire net) and make the express line even more efficient and fast-moving. The next thing you know, Fear always gets moved to the head of the line and we've essentially *wired ourselves for fear* in our brain's neural network. In the words of Donald Hebb (a Canadian behavioral neuropsychologist): "what fires together, wires together."

But don't worry. After reading this chapter you might be tempted to say: "Oh no! I'm doomed to have a fearFULL brain because I've spent most, if not all, of my life reacting with fear to stressors and now my brain is permanently wired for fear". As I'll explain shortly, we have an amazing brain fully able to rewire itself. You can build new, more adaptive neural pathways by doing the work necessary to make new fearLESS neural connections. You can actually change your "brain bank account" and subdue your amygdala through conscious effort. Just know that you'll never be able to switch off your amygdala; no one can. The amygdala has survived in humans and other species over millions of years of evolution because it serves a definite survival purpose.

So the good news is that we're not slaves to our fears. We can take advantage of the fact that we can change the neural pathways in our brain — create new healthy neural networks — simply by changing our behavior and thought processes (a concept referred to as neuroplasticity of the brain). We can actually take control of our relationship with Fear and eventually become the one with the power, not him. But we'll get to that in a bit. Right now let's keep our focus on the consequences of fear on our internal systems.

Chapter Five
Fear and Our Body Systems

"Heavy thoughts bring on physical maladies; when the soul is
oppressed so is the body."
Martin Luther

"Over the years your bodies become walking autobiographies, telling
friends and strangers alike of the minor and major stresses of your life."
Marilyn Ferguson

Fear doesn't just leave an imprint in our brain; no indeed.
Fear also leaves an imprint on our body. This is yet another way
in which he puts up barriers between us and our freedom to live
the life we deserve. How does having a dysfunctional
relationship with fear have consequences for our body? Well, as
you've learned in Chapter Two, fear is a form of stress and living
with stress — particularly the chronic stress that comes with
habitually responding to life's challenges with fear — often has
definite physical health consequences. Since we discussed
chronic stress in Chapter Two, I'll focus here on Fear's impact
on our internal system; particularly how he uses our sympathetic
nervous system to wreak havoc on our body, right down to the
cellular level.

This is how it works. When we're faced with a threat (a
stressor), our brain makes us to want to take some immediate
action; to flight or run away. Our brain prepares us
psychologically by increasing the activity in the amygdala and
hippocampus but also prepares us *physically* by releasing stress
hormones such as adrenaline and cortisol right into our blood

stream. It does this by sending signals to nerve cells to release these chemicals in order to start a series of changes in our body.

Our *sympathetic* nervous system is our fight-or-flight centre and automatically releases these hormones to prepare our body to become physically alert and ready to deal with the threat. We sweat; our breathing becomes rapid as our respiratory rate increases; our impulses quicken; and, our muscles and limbs tighten as more blood rushes into them to get them fuelled and ready for action. We get goose bumps as adrenaline causes the hair follicles to stand up from our skin (a phenomenon referred to as piloerection). Even our vision improves as our pupils dilate with our heightened awareness of the identified threat; we get what's often called tunnel vision as we focus entirely on the threat at hand.

Have you ever noticed how fear is depicted in cartoons? In general, the character that is experiencing fear is shown with huge eyes, a heart that's thumping out from the character's chest and hair that's standing on end. Although this is a gross exaggeration, it's based on our real-life human physical reactions when we interpret a situation as stressful and experience fear as a response.

We don't even have to think about our fight-or-flight response — it's an instinctive, automatic, and unconscious reaction that we never have to actually bring to the conscious level before it takes effect (remember, our amygdala is in charge when we're in fight-or-flight mode). While we're in this state of arousal, besides the activity happening in our brain, other things in our body under the control of our *parasympathetic* nervous system (responsible for relaxation and what some have referred to as the "rest and digest" activities of the body), is halted or slowed down as we focus with laser-like precision on the threat.

For example, our digestive system slows down as our body redirects blood to our muscles in preparation for fight or flight.

Whether we fight or flee from a physical threat, we perform some action. This physical action is actually good for us because the energy expended when we fight or run away helps our body get rid of the stress hormones that have built up in our system when the threat emerged. Once the threat is gone, our immediate sense of fear goes away as well (although the threat and our reaction is now stored in our memory and, if we focus on the memory, our sympathetic nervous system can keep us in a state of alertness, looking out for the next possible source of threat). Our parasympathetic nervous system kicks back into gear and we go back to normal breathing with a regular heart rate, lose the tension in our muscles and our bladders, and our bowels get back to work. We've completed the fight-or-flight response cycle and our bodies get back to a state referred to as *homeostasis* when our system is in balance.

Our Fight-or-Flight Response Cycle

Cognitive (Thinking)	Physiological (Unconscious)	Emotional (Feeling)	Behavioral → (Action)
• Perception of a threat (real or imagined)	• Increased heart rate • Digestive system slows down	• Feeling of fear or anger or other stress-related emotion	• Flight (run away from the source of fear) • Fight (confront the source of fear)

However, as you now know, most of our threats today don't come in a physical form. Most of our threats are emotional or psychological in nature and are caused when people (e.g., criticism from a husband or wife; disrespectful treatment by a boss or co-worker, a snarky comment or insult from a friend) or circumstances (e.g., being asked to give a public speech; being stuck in traffic when you're already late for an appointment; unreasonably tight work or school deadlines) cause us to feel "stressed out", threatened, anxious, or fearful. That is, we perceive what has happened, or about to happen, to us as stressful and we might react with fear, anxiety or other emotional response.

FEAR FACT #21: Fear makes sure your brain sends the same fight-flight messages to your body regardless of whether you're reacting to a physical or emotional stressor.

Fear knows very well that our brain and sympathetic and parasympathetic nervous system cause us to react the same way to a physical threat as we would react to an emotional threat. That is, our reaction to the emotional threat also makes us want to fight or run away. But, although emotional stressors or threats cause the exact same fear response that physical stressors do, the difference lies in what we can do about the threat.

Fear Keeps Us Off-Balance

By its very nature, fear forces us to deal with it. In the case of physical threats, we can run away or fight to protect ourselves. But we can't really do that with emotional or psychological threats. We can't punch the overly demanding boss who criticizes our best efforts or the cashier who chats with her co-worker and keeps us standing in a long line at the checkout counter while our ice cream melts in our grocery cart. We can't ram the car ahead of us because the driver keeps tapping the breaks or lash out at the colleague who is the office bully and insists on getting his own way on every corporate team project.

So, when we're faced with emotional or psychological threats, rather than performing some action (as we would do when faced with a physical threat), we generally have to stay and take it. We tend to have to stay in the presence of the threat (like working for the same inconsiderate boss or waiting for the same irritating cashier) far longer than is good for our emotional and physical health.

In today's modern society, we have an accumulation of these threats to our well-being, many of which trigger our fight-or-flight response. As such, we get ongoing exposure to things that make us feel angry, fearful, resentful or anxious and the stress hormones accumulate in our body. When we're in a dysfunctional relationship with Fear, he makes sure that our amygdala is primed and ready to fight or flee much of the time given that we're likely to encounter something or someone that causes us to feel threatened or stressed. In other words, Fear keeps our fight-or-flight switched set to "ON" most of the time. We become primed to perceive threats, even in situations that other people may not find threatening or stressful.

Our bodies haven't been designed to deal with ongoing threats that cause us to feel fearful, anxious or angry, especially when we have to bottle up our emotions and remain in the presence of the stressor that's causing us to feel stress or fear. Our bodies have been designed to handle acute stress and fears so that we can quickly go through the fight-or-flight response cycle and get back to a relaxed state.

When we deal with prolonged exposure to stressors, like those that cause us to have a fear response, Fear takes control of our brain and our brain constantly bombards our body with messages of fight-or-flight. This in turn causes our heart, lungs, blood vessels and muscles to become chronically over-activated. As a result, the stress hormones that build up in our bodies over time as a result of being exposed to these stressors have nowhere to go. We don't burn off the effects of the stress hormones and therefore can't complete the flight-fight response cycle that we've been genetically programmed to do.

FEAR FACT #22: Fear keeps you in fight-fight mode which makes you vulnerable to acute and chronic physical illnesses.

This wreaks havoc with our body as I discussed in Chapter Two. We end up with an increased risk for heart disease, cancer, stroke, asthma, ulcers, digestive problems, high blood pressure, fertility and sexual dysfunctions, skin problems, irritable bowel syndrome, kidney disease, allergies, obesity, headaches, memory loss and a host of other acute or chronic illnesses.

The long term effect of chronic emotional stress that comes from an ongoing dysfunctional relationship with Fear is even more harmful than purely physical threats. This is due to the fact that years of constantly giving in to our fears will gradually erode our body's natural ability to cope. This, in turn, will make us vulnerable to disease and other physical health issues. But even more importantly, our fear response to stressors and physical health problems has a feedback loop; they reinforce each other.

How does the feedback loop work? When someone habitually reacts to a stressor with fear, their body can eventually break down under the weight of this chronic stress. One of the ways that their body can break down is when they get an acute or chronic physical illness. When the person experiences symptoms or gets a diagnosis that they have a physical illness, this is a new source of stress and fear for them. This new source of stress now contributes to their original stress and fear response, often making it worse. This chain of cause and effect causes a circuit or feedback loop that can increase the original level of the person's fear and the severity of their physical illness.

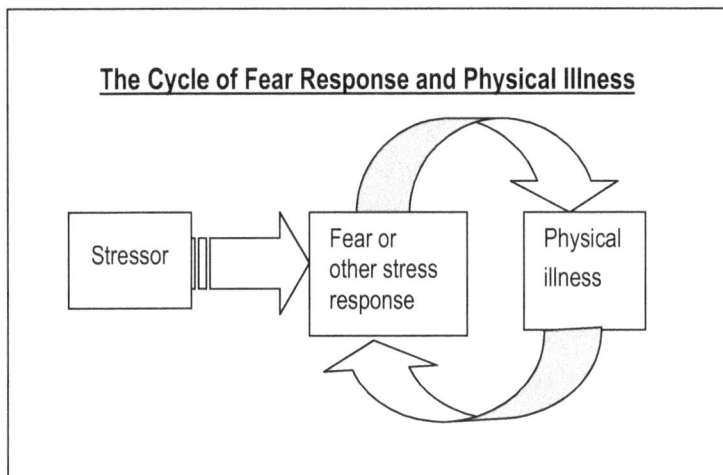

The Cycle of Fear Response and Physical Illness

| Stressor | → | Fear or other stress response | Physical illness |

Physical illness begins right down at the cellular level. Remember I said that we're surrounded by systems, both external and internal? Well, the human body is itself a system — a collection of cells working together to perform a common function. Our body system needs to be stable and balanced (i.e., homeostasis) in order for it to function properly. However, Fear does his best to interfere with our body's ability to balance and function properly. One of the ways he does this is by upsetting the flow of energy to our cells.

Each and every cell in our body relies on energy to function properly. If the cell is deficient in energy, it can't contribute to the other internal systems in our body (e.g., cardiovascular system; digestive system, reproductive system, etc.) that it has been designed to function in. When the body is continually stressed (like when someone habitually responds to stressors with fear), it doesn't produce energy as well and becomes energy-deficient. Over time the body becomes less efficient and damaged. Some of its internal systems may even slow down or stop some of their functions in order to conserve energy. This can result in cell damage or even cell death.

When Fear challenges our internal systems by constantly setting our fight-or-flight switch to "ON", it puts a burden on our body. Our body is never at rest, never peaceful, as long as we're in a dysfunctional relationship with Fear. As the stress hormones flood our body over time, it struggles to adapt and heal itself in order to get back to a stable internal environment. Being in a continual state of fear prevents our body from appropriately managing its systems. In fact, our body's attempts to compensate and adjust can actually make the situation worse. Research has shown, for example, that the body's sensors are often damaged during periods of prolonged stress. Damaged sensors are less able to make the proper adjustments to get our body back to a state of balance and this may cause further cell damage.

When we're in an ongoing dysfunctional relationship with Fear, our body will do it's best to protect our internal systems and maintain balance. However, while our body is working to get back to a state of balance, Fear is working to keep it in a state of imbalance. Fear and imbalance are at opposite ends of the spectrum — we can't experience fear (that is, a state of fight-or-flight) and have our body be in a state of balance and rest at the same time.

Because of the harmful effects of emotional stress such as a habitual fear response to stressors, you need to pay attention to what your body may be telling you. Even if you think you're managing your fear your body may be telling you something entirely different. That's because you don't need to be experiencing a full-blown fear reaction to be experiencing fear at a physiological level. Your fear reaction can go directly to your body and cause damage even without your conscious awareness of feeling threatened.

You learned a bit in Chapter Two, and will learn more in Chapter Twelve, that one important part of dealing with your fears is the identification of your fear triggers. When your stomach is continually upset, or you have recurring headaches or muscle tension, a racing heartbeat, shallow breathing or grinding your teeth, your body is telling you that something is not right with your internal systems and that you're in a state of imbalance.

But again, don't be alarmed. You aren't doomed to suffer the harmful effects of fear on your body, just as you're not doomed to suffer the harmful effects of fear on your brain. Although your sympathetic nervous system is hierarchically dominant to your parasympathetic nervous system (that is, your amygdala can tell your prefrontal cortex to take a back seat while it deals with a perceived threat), you can still *take control of your perception and reaction* to things or situations that might cause you to feel fear. But, as you'll see later, it will take a conscious effort on your part to do so.

Chapter Six
Fear and Our Mind Systems

"The mind is the greatest power in all of creation."
J.B. Rhine

"Our mind can be our greatest asset or our greatest hindrance."
Jacinth Tracey

"The brain carries out what the mind wants. To mistake the brain, a lump of proteins, sugar and water, for a mind is a drastic mistake."
Deepak Chopra

You now know that habitual fear reactions to stress triggers can do real harm to your brain and your body. But did you know that Fear has one more trick up his sleeve; that he has one more way to create barriers between you and the fearLESS life you want to live? Taking control of your mind is the third and most efficient way that Fear exerts control over your life. Your mind, particularly your subconscious mind, is the ultimate control centre and when Fear is in control of your mind, he's able to control your destiny.

At this point you might be asking yourself: "The mind? Isn't the mind and brain the same thing?" The short answer is no they are not. The brain and the mind are two separate entities; the *brain is a physical entity* and the *mind is a nonphysical entity*. We can see the brain with the naked eye (e.g., during brain surgery or after it's been exposed due to a traumatic head injury) or by using x-rays or various types of imaging scans. However, the mind is something that can't be seen with the naked eye or with any type of imaging technology. That's because the mind doesn't actually have any physical properties; it's not located at one specific place in our body but instead *functions in every single cell in our body*. The mind is extremely powerful; in fact it's the most powerful tool we'll ever have and all that we'll ever need to overcome our fears because it's what controls both our brain and our body.

People differ significantly in how well-attuned they are to their own mind system, particularly what might be going on in their subconscious mind. Asking them to reflect on their own behavior isn't always helpful; they can't always make the right *cognitive appraisals*. That's because we don't always have insight into our own behavior or our feelings. For example, someone might be calmly going through their day when suddenly they feel their heart racing, their stomach clenching and their hands shaking. Or they might suddenly feel sad and tearful with a foreboding sense that something unpleasant was going to happen. Out of nowhere they begin to experience fight-or-flight arousal symptoms and, as they look around, they don't see anything that might be causing them to react this way. If there was something obvious, say a speeding car heading in their direction, then it would be easy to make a causal attribution. The person would look at the speeding car (a stressor) and say to themself "Aha! That's why I feel afraid" and take the appropriate action to get out of the way. But what could possibly be going on when they don't "see" anything? Why don't we always know why we're feeling fearful?

You now know that fear reactions are triggered when our amygdala fires out signals to fight or flee from a stressor. But where is our amygdala getting that information from when we can't "see" any threat or don't even remember thinking about something that would make us feel fearful? What's going on in our brain? Is it independently, of its own accord, sending fight-

or-flight signals to our body? Of course not. Our brain is getting that information from somewhere and that somewhere is our mind. Our mind, particularly our subconscious mind, can interpret something as a fear trigger and instruct our brain to begin the fight-or-flight reaction even when we're not consciously aware of any imminent threat. That's because much of the information we take in from our external environment occurs subliminally (i.e., below our level of conscious awareness).

Our brain is the control center of our central nervous system, but our mind is the control center of all that we are and all that we will ever be. It's the real powerhouse controlling how we think, feel and behave. In that sense, our mind is superior to our brain and actually controls and informs our brain which in turns controls and informs our body.

FEAR FACT #23: Your mind is the ultimate control centre and guides everything you think, feel, say and do. All your fears originate in your mind. The brain is secondary to the mind.

This is how it works. Our mind is related to our brain; it interacts with our brain but is a separate entity. As I discussed earlier, our brain consists of physical matter but our mind is non-physical. Although science doesn't understand exactly how our non-physical mind can interact with and control our physical brain, it's generally agreed that our mind is the thing that allows us to have self-awareness and to make distinctions in how we perceive and respond to our physical and social environment.

There's scientific proof that our mind affects our brain. When people are asked to think about certain things, like reflecting on a specific memory or visualizing a specific image, their brain activity changes. As well, experiments using placebos (i.e., fake medication usually in the form of a sugar pill) have shown that people who believed that they were taking a brain modifying pill were actually able to change their brain's physiological and chemical activity. In these mind-brain experiments, the fact that people simply *believed and expected* that the pill they'd taken was real medicine was enough to create changes in their brain even though no brain modifying medication was actually used. In fact, it's been reported that, on average, the mind-brain power of placebos are responsible for up to one-third of all improvements from treatments in many drug studies. These mind-brain studies show that changes in our brain can be triggered simply by the intentions of our mind. These types of studies provide indisputable evidence of the power of our mind over our brain.

Our Conscious and Subconscious Mind

Our mind is where we store *everything* about our experiences, and how we view ourselves and our relationship with the physical and social world (i.e., our external systems). It's where our thoughts reside and where our *consciousness* lies; that is, our subjective awareness of ourselves and our place in the world. We use our mind to reflect on our behaviors and thoughts, and to initiate changes if we don't like what we're thinking or the way we're behaving. Whenever we're having private conversations in our head (called *self-talk* or *talking to ourselves*) we're using our mind.

This feature of the mind is what many believe makes us inherently human and distinct and unique from all other species — the fact that not only do we have a brain, but we have an evolved mind. Let's take the example of a puppy and a baby; both are looking in a mirror. Both have a brain and eyes and sensory receptors that let them perceive an image reflecting back at them. At 6 months old, both the puppy and the baby will look at their image in the mirror and have no idea that the image looking back at them is actually a physical reflection of themselves. They're both aware of their own body and their physical and social environment but neither is *self-aware*. That is, they can't "see" themselves as a unique object in the world, apart from other people, or in terms of their traits, feelings and behaviors.

By the time the child gets to be about 3 years-old however she has developed self-awareness; she has the power of introspection. She now knows that the reflection in the mirror is her own image. In fact, she can also distinguish her own image from among other images that might be reflecting back at her in that mirror. Based on her perception of herself, she can also make a subjective self-appraisal by comparing herself to others in her social group (e.g., her friends, family, or other girls she sees on television or in magazines). By comparing herself to others she can decide if she feels good or bad about herself and adjust her thoughts, feelings and her behavior accordingly. However, no matter how old the dog gets, he'll never be able to reflect on himself or his own thoughts or make any conscious attempt to adjust his thoughts or behavior. He will never be self-aware. Our mind, therefore, is our greatest human asset; it's where we give meaning to our life and to the world around us. It's where we can begin to make the changes we want to see happen in our lives, and how we actually begin shape our lives to reflect our own unique dreams and goals.

Just like our brain system has different areas that have specialized functions (like the amygdala, hippocampus and prefrontal cortex), our mind system also has specialized areas and functions. Our mind is divided into two parts: our conscious mind and our subconscious mind. *Our conscious mind is our "thinking mind" and our subconscious mind is our "emotional mind"*.

Let me create an image for you. Picture your mind like an iceberg. Like all icebergs, what you're able to see on the surface is only a small portion of the size of the iceberg itself. Most of the mass — in fact about 90% — of the iceberg can't be seen because it lies below the surface of the water. It's the same way with your mind. You can think of your conscious mind as the tip of the iceberg; what you can see above the surface. But the greater part of your mind lies in your subconscious; which lies unseen beneath the surface.

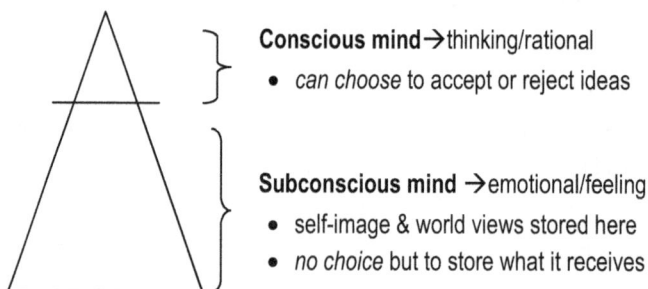

Conscious mind →thinking/rational
- *can choose* to accept or reject ideas

Subconscious mind →emotional/feeling
- self-image & world views stored here
- *no choice* but to store what it receives

As you can see from the diagram, our conscious mind takes up a smaller part of our mind system. It's the part of our mind where we can *consciously and deliberately choose to think certain things about ourselves and our physical and social environment*. As we go through life, we're taking in information from our social and physical environments. This information from the outside world (i.e., our external systems) comes to us from our senses (i.e., see, hear, touch, smell and taste) and is assimilated by our conscious thought processes. You learned earlier that our thought processes can be mapped to the prefrontal cortex portion of our brain. Now you know that thought processes also happen in our conscious mind as well.

Our conscious mind takes in information from our external environment as we go through life and can accept or reject any idea or information we put into it. Did you know that no matter what happens to us in life, we're actually making choices about how we deal with it? Specifically, how we interpret or think about what happens to us is based on two things: 1) our past conditioning; and, 2) the *meaning* we give to the experience based on the memories held in our subconscious mind which are filtered through our conscious mind. Whenever we're presented with a stressor, for example, we can choose to think positive things (like "I'm capable of handling my fears. I'm in control and won't let this get to me") or we can choose to think negative things (like "I can't get over my fears. I can't control the things that happen to me").

Whatever information we take in from our external systems is stored in our physical brain (our hippocampus), but more importantly our memory also gets stored in our subconscious mind where it's added to the other stored memories to help form our attitudes, beliefs and values about ourselves and the world. But unlike our brain's hippocampus which has a limited storage space (remember, it stores our life experiences into short-term and long-term memory; particularly the "memorable memories" that were triggered by our amygdala), our subconscious mind has unlimited storage space and stores all types of information, not just the emotional-based "memorable memories".

You can think of our hippocampus as storing all the information we could physically carry around with us, like putting a few file folders in a briefcase. But our subconscious mind is like an infinite filing cabinet, storing file folders with information on every single thing we've ever thought, felt, seen, said and done. It holds every memory we'll ever have as well as the emotions associated with those memories.

In fact, our subconscious mind is the ultimate recording machine; it videotapes and audiotapes every bit of information that we send to it. All the childhood conditioning, all the media conditioning, all the things that we've accepted as true about ourselves are alive and well, and living in our subconscious mind. While on a conscious level we choose what we think about, our subconscious mind is busy storing *all* our thoughts and feelings — it has no choice. So that means that *whatever you've chosen to believe about yourself* (through the conditioning of your brain and your conscious mind) *is always accepted by your subconscious mind*; it has no choice but to accept what it's being told.

FEAR FACT #24: What you've told yourself about what you fear and your ability to overcome your fear is deeply embedded not only in your brain, but more importantly, in your subconscious mind which always accepts the information you give it.

As you can see from the previous diagram, our subconscious mind, like the iceberg, takes up the greater portion of our mind. Like the iceberg, many believe that the subconscious mind is responsible for 90% of the feelings, values and habitual behavior patterns that we acquired through our direct and indirect conditioning (yes; that means that almost everything we do and feel is not under our immediate conscious control). Every time we've interacted with our physical or social environment; every time we ate, saw, touched or heard something, or heard about someone else's experience, the memory and the feelings associated with it has been stored and accumulating in our subconscious mind. Every time we've had a fear reaction to a stressor, it got stored as a "memory deposit" in our subconscious mind.

Our conscious and subconscious mind work together as a system to create our *paradigm*. Our paradigm is essentially the way we habitually way think, feel and behave. Because our subconscious mind is entirely emotional, the memories it contains have to be filtered through our conscious, thinking mind in order to inject logic and reason and give our memories meaning. If the memories in our subconscious mind wasn't filtered through our conscious mind our memories would just be a jumbled mess of images and emotions that we couldn't make sense of and learn from.

As you learned in the previous chapter our brain's amygdala and hippocampus work together to provide meaning to our experiences. However, the emotional component of that meaning is under the control of our subconscious mind. This is a very important distinction because it's the *emotional meaning* that we attach to the memories held in our subconscious mind that causes us to falter or achieve success in life. It's the meaning that we give to our memories — how we classify them as negative or positive, challenges or opportunities, failures or lessons-learned — that determines whether we approach life full of fear of full of empowerment.

Your subconscious mind holds the key to how you view yourself and the life you've lived, but more importantly it holds the key to how you view your ability to gain control and achieve your personal power. Working to build a stronger and more deliberate relationship between your conscious and subconscious mind will highlight where there are any differences between your thinking/rational conscious mind and your emotional/feeling subconscious mind. By strengthening this relationship you'll be able to learn more about yourself and what drives your thoughts, feelings and actions. This is a necessary step for you to overcome your fears and get the successful life that you want. When you take the time to ask yourself key questions about your own beliefs about yourself, and to evaluate whether or not there's consistent, objective evidence to support your beliefs, you'll begin to see the connection between your paradigm and your life outcomes.

Some questions you may want to ask yourself at this point are:

1. What do I believe about myself, and why do I believe those things?
2. How do I feel when I think certain negative things about myself?
3. How do I feel when I think certain positive things about myself?
4. How do these feelings and my beliefs about myself cause me to act in certain ways?
5. What objective evidence do I have to support that the beliefs and feelings that I have about myself are a true reflection of who I really am at my core?

The things we say and do (i.e., our behavior) is *external* but the foundation of our behavior, particularly our emotional behavior (like our fears) is *internal*. Other people can observe *what* we say or do, but they can only guess *why* we act a certain way or say certain things. No one else can know what it feels like to be any other person. The only insight that anyone can get about what might be going on in someone else's mind is what the person consciously or subconsciously communicates to them through the things they do or the things they say. That's because things like motivation and emotional states lie deep within our mind. No one else can access our mind unless we let them. Even you, if you don't know how your mind works, have very little awareness about why you habitually behave in certain ways or are "always" saying the wrong things or thinking negative, fearFULL thoughts.

So many of my clients during their first appointment with me say things like: "I don't know why I do the things I do" or "I don't know why I can't seem to control myself" or "I don't know what's wrong with me" or "I don't know why the same bad things keep happening to me all the time". That is, they look at the consequences of their behavior (e.g., problems with fear, problems with anger or guilt, problems with their personal or professional life, etc.) but don't have any real insight or have never really reflected on the internal drivers for their emotions, thoughts and behaviors. They only know, for example, that they feel sad, anxious, depressed, fearful, angry or frustrated and can't seem to get beyond their own limitations. Or they assume that they know the cause of their fears but still aren't able to overcome them despite their attempts. In either case, they can't move forward and can't seem to get out of their own way. That's because they're largely unaware of the power of their subconscious mind on their thoughts and behaviors, and ultimately their life outcomes. They don't realize that the thoughts being generated in their subconscious mind is driving their fears and their inability to succeed in life.

Like everyone else, you've been taking in and processing information consciously and subconsciously since the day you were born. Repeating negative things and experiences in your head, like fearful reactions to stressors, wires not only your brain but your subconscious mind as well. The more you think fearful thoughts and perform fearful actions (fight-or-flight), you're actually leaving a physical trace in the neural pathways in your brain (amygdala and hippocampus) but, more importantly, you're leaving an emotional trace in your subconscious mind. In fact, the memories of your previous fear responses to stress triggers accumulate in your subconscious mind and add to the existing impression that you already have of yourself as a fearful person. Remember, your subconscious mind can only reflect back to you the information you send it.

Let's think of it another way. If your subconscious mind is a hard drive on your computer (storing all your programs and data) then your conscious mind is the computer monitor. What appears on the monitor is only a fraction of all the information that's stored on the hard drive. Plus, what appears on the monitor depends entirely on what information you choose to pull up from your computer's hard drive.

But guess what? You're the one who gets to decide what type of information you want to pull from your hard drive. Do you want to pull up fearFULL information and paradigms that'll keep you helpless to overcome your fear barriers or do you want to install and pull up fearLESS programs that will move you towards fulfilling your dreams of a successful life? Constantly putting the same fearful, negative information into your subconscious mind will make fearful, negative thinking and behavior *automatic*. Your fear programs will load automatically without you even making a conscious effort to call them up from your subconscious mind. In other words, you won't even have to consciously think a fearful thought but it'll still affect your outlook and how you respond to your physical and social environment.

How does that happen you might be asking yourself? Well, you acquired your fears through the direct and indirect conditioning that occurred in your brain and your mind. Either you, or someone in your environment, taught you to fear something or some situation and that has impacted your thoughts, feelings and your behavior. So, when you encounter that something or situation, you think, feel and respond with fear. That's because your brain's neural networks recognizes a familiar wired-in pattern of responding and your subconscious mind automatically tells your brain what you feel about the stressor based on your established self-perceptions about your ability to cope.

> **FEAR FACT #25:** Over time your fearful response to stressors becomes automatic and mindless; bypassing your conscious mind, because you've wired your brain and subconscious mind for fear.

Let's take a driving example. When someone first learns to drive a car it takes a lot of conscious mental activity. They have to remember to keep their hands in the correct position on the steering wheel, and have to be alert about how hard their foot is pressing on the gas pedal so that they don't go too fast or too slow for the posted speed limit. And they likely can't hold a conversation with any passengers because all of their conscious attention and mental effort is focused on the mechanics of their driving.

Fast-forward to a few years later. That person now drives from A to B without much conscious mental effort at all. In fact, they likely get into their car, navigate their way through rush hour traffic stopping at all the red lights and signaling appropriately, keep up a running chatter with their passengers, and get home safely with no real memory of having focused any attention on the mechanics of driving at all.

When they first started driving it took conscious effort, but over the years of repeated driving all the mechanics of driving had become subconscious. They practiced their driving skills and now those skills have become automatic. This has freed their conscious mind to focus on other things while they're driving. They're still a safe driver because their excellent driving skills are now part of their subconscious mind even when they aren't focusing on the mechanics of driving at a conscious level. Their subconscious is guiding their behavior (and determining their results) with very little conscious effort on their part.

This is the same way that fear works in your life. You've practiced your fears (through your habitual fear-responses) and now your fear response to stressors have become automatic. They've become automatic because you've wired a fear neural net in your brain, but more importantly you've wired your subconscious mind for fear. Your fears can now affect you even when you're not consciously aware of what's happening because they can come from your subconscious mind and can guide your thoughts and behavior without any conscious effort on your part at all. Like most people, your fears are in the drivers' seat, not you. And they're taking you down dead-end roads and on life detours that prevent you from getting to the successful life that you want.

Our subconscious mind is where we store ideas about how we view the world, and more specifically, how we view ourselves (i.e., our self-image). It plays the biggest role in the maintenance of our fears. That's because what we fear, and how we react to fear triggers, is based on the way we see ourselves. Fear knows very well that our level of self-awareness and our self-image is crucial to our ability to overcome fear barriers. That's why he works so hard to warp and distort our self-image and keep us from growing in our self-awareness. He knows that if he can do this, he can have ultimate control of what we think (our brain and conscious mind) and what we do (our body and actions) and ultimately have control over our life outcomes.

Self-awareness plays a large part of what's often referred to as *mindfulness*. In order to be mindful, you need to be aware of yourself and the things you're doing while you're doing them.

Mindfulness has been defined in many ways including:
- Paying conscious attention to what you're paying attention to (or paying attention on purpose).
- Being of the moment, for the moment, in the moment (not thinking about the past or the future).
- Experiencing, not judging, what's happening to you and what you're feeling (seeing yourself from the viewpoint of an impartial observer).

For example, like most of us, you probably go through life hardly paying attention to the things that have become automatic for you. Take eating for example. When was the last time that you purposely paid attention to what and how you were eating while you were eating your meal? Like most of us, you probably eat your meals while doing other tasks (e.g., working at your desk; having a conversation with someone; watching television, thinking about what you did earlier or what you need to do later; etc.) and really don't focus on the actual act of eating. That is, you don't really notice the texture of your food, how different bites feel against your taste buds, or how it feels to swallow. This can be referred to as mindless eating; where only a small part of you is aware of what you're doing; the rest of you is on automatic.

But when you're eating mindfully, you try to purposely pay attention to the act of eating while you're eating. If your mind wanders or you get distracted, you purposely bring your awareness and attention back to what you're doing. That way, you're aware of what you're eating and how much you're eating and can stop yourself before you overeat. You also appreciate your meal much better as you focus on the taste and texture and smell of it.

One of the way Fear keeps our fear response on automatic is that he prevents us from being self-aware; prevents us from being mindful. We're each so busy mindlessly responding to life the way he wants us to that we're really not paying conscious attention to what's happening. We're in reaction mode and don't take the time to notice or re-direct and focus our attention to other possible ways of seeing ourselves or perceiving the situation that's causing us to feel fearful. We approach each situation, or experience each threat, based on past experiences and fearful that that's how it'll always be. The present moment is overshadowed by fearful shadows of the past and ghosts of the future. We aren't "present" in our experience, we're on automatic. Fear causes us to interpret and judge everything we experience from a fear-based automatic, mindless, conditioned perspective.

Fear makes Us Feel Limited

I've always been fascinated by animals, both wild and domestic. When I was a child, I'd eagerly look forward to the weekend when Wild Kingdom would be on television and would be riveted by the colorful pictures of animals in the National Geographic magazine. To this day I like to spend some of my leisure time watching television programs that allow me to see various animals and learn about different species and their habitats.

One of the things that I've noticed is how some animals behave after they've been rescued and rehabilitated. For example, after some horrible industrial oil spill or natural disaster, some animals need human help to survive; to wash the sticky oil off their fur or feathers, or to mend a broken wing or leg. The animals that can't be quickly cleaned up and released, or are in serious condition and need more time to get treated, are held in captivity for a while so that they can heal. Once they've been nursed back to health, their caregivers are overjoyed and eager to release them back into their natural environment. So they take the animal in its cage right back to where it was found and open the cage door.

Now you'd think that that animal would bolt right out of the cage once the door was opened, right? After all, beyond the boundaries of the cage lies freedom. The animal can do whatever it wants once it gets out of that cage; it can spread its wings or stretch its legs and roam freely. But you might be surprised to learn that many animals don't bolt from the cage to freedom at all. In fact they do the opposite; they looked fearfully out of the cage door and hunker down, unwilling to take a step forward. Even with coaxing and encouragement from their caregivers, the animal stays put, refusing to budge. What's going on? That doesn't seem to make any sense.

This is what happened. When the animal was first captured it had no idea that the humans were there to help. Its natural instinct likely told it that the human trying to catch it was a threat. That perception, even though it was false, initiated the animal's fight-or-flight response and it wanted to run or fight back for fear of its life. But because it was injured and couldn't escape; it was helpless. So it was captured and put in a cage so that it wouldn't hurt itself while it was getting treated for its injuries.

Deprived of its natural ability to roam freely, the animal learned that it had little or no control; that it had very limited boundaries. Even though it was an initially unpleasant and negative feeling, that feeling of having little control and limited boundaries became familiar to the animal. So, days or months later when it was healed and given the opportunity to get out of the cage, it didn't do that. That's because the animal had adopted a *limiting belief* that the confines of the cage was as far as it could ever hope to go. Limiting beliefs are formed as a result of experiencing a painful or negative experience. It's only when the caregiver shows the animal that it's free by continuing to coax it out of the corner of the cage or by taking it out and placing it outside the cage, that the animal can "see" that the door is wide open; that it's free to run or fly away to enjoy the life it was meant to live.

FEAR FACT #26: Fear makes you feel that there are limits to what you can do in your life. In reality, there are no limits, only the ones you place on yourself.

That's exactly how our dysfunctional relationship with Fear works. He places limits on our thoughts, emotions and actions. We eventually come to believe that those limits are actually real and live our life, and think thoughts according to those tight boundaries. We automatically and mindlessly, think, feel and act as if there's only so much room for us to maneuver in our life. In reality nothing could be further from the truth; we really have no limits at all. Our perception of limits is an illusion.

Your conditioning has caused your limiting beliefs, and your dysfunctional relationship with Fear keeps those limiting beliefs flowing into your subconscious mind. Now these limits have been wired deep within your brain and subconscious mind and you can't be free to explore who you really are; you have no freedom of thought or of movement. Your false beliefs cause you to live a life of default rather than a life of our own design. You go with the flow, even when the flow is pushing you downstream, rather than taking control and heading in a direction of your own choosing. Your false beliefs and misperceptions that stem from the information you've put into our subconscious mind prevent you from seeing that you're already free to move beyond the cage of your own misperceptions. But Fear puts blinders on you; he doesn't want you to see the unlimited possibilities. He wants to keep you caged.

One of the greatest joys that I have as a transformational coach and mindset mentor is that I get to help people see and move beyond their self-imposed cages. Take Denise for example. I met her over 20 years ago when she was suffering from poor self-esteem due to a 6-inch vertical scar running down the front of her lower leg. She was allowing that scar to cloud her entire judgment about her attractiveness and self worth. In fact, she'd wear thick, dark stockings or pants even in the heat of summer. It took a few sessions before she would even let me see the scar. Her poor self-esteem was affecting her relationship with her husband and her ability to assert herself at work. She was so submissive and spoke so softly that oftentimes it was hard to hear her. Whenever she laughed, which was seldom, she would cover her mouth with her hands and hang her head.

Denise had allowed her scar, and the fear of being judged negatively or rejected because of it, to place limits not only on what she wore, but how she thought about herself. Her negative self-image and lack of self-awareness was causing her to live a very limited life. Although she was unhappy with the emotionally abusive and dismissive way her husband treated her, and the fact that she couldn't get the courage to ask for a much-deserved raise at work, she was fearful about asserting herself. At the heart of Denise's reluctance was a feeling of powerlessness over her personal and professional life. She had let her dysfunctional relationship with Fear put limits on how she saw herself and her ability to control her own life.

After helping her to transform her mind and her brain, Denise's life changed. She began to see herself in a new light. She began to define herself not by the self-imposed limits caused by that scar, but by all her other wonderful qualities that she had ignored because of her dysfunctional relationship with Fear. She initially began wearing skirts with lighter-colored stockings, and eventually progressed to wearing skirts without any stockings at all.

She'd spent the previous 15 years hiding a scar, and herself, from the world for fear that she would be rejected or judged negatively. No longer caged by her fear, the increase in self-esteem that came with her transformation also flowed into her personal and professional life. Her happiness increased significantly as did her self-awareness about the power of her subconscious mind to either view her scar negatively or to view it as simply a part of her body; without any judgment. Even 20 years later, Denise still tells me whenever I happen to run into her about how grateful she is that I "fixed" her, as she describes it. I always remind her that it was she who fixed herself; I was simply the person who provided her with the proper tools to do so.

Are you allowing your dysfunctional relationship with Fear to keep you caged to a limited life? Do you see yourself as "less than" because of something you view as an imperfection? Do you see something in your character or in your physical appearance as a fatal flaw? Do you feel that you lack the intelligence, the talent or the skills to move ahead in your life? Just know that the boundaries that you're placing on yourself are an illusion caused by limiting beliefs. Fear is using that illusion to keep you in an ongoing, dependent, dysfunctional relationship with him.

Like Denise before her transformation, when you look at your world with a fearful mind you have a false and biased view of what the world has to offer and your ability to exert control over your life. You live your life in a tiny self-imposed cage of doubt and fear oblivious to the vast world of freedom and choice right in front of you. It's only when you take the leap of faith and step out of that cage that Fear has placed you in that you truly step into your power and see the freedom that you have to choose and get the life you want.

Fear makes Us Feel Helpless

One of my favorite images, and one that I often share with clients, is a picture of a large elephant held in place on the grass by a tiny rope placed around one of its front legs. The other end of the rope is tied to a small stick stuck into the grass. In that picture the elephant is clearly unhappy and is looking out across the grass to the great expanse of forest in front of it. The elephant has enough physical strength and power to easily break his bonds but instead stays in place. Why is that? Why doesn't he just take a step forward, break free, and run to the forest that he can clearly see in front of him?

The reason he doesn't break free is that he's being held captive. However, it's not the rope that holds him captive; it's the conditioning of his mind. You see, it was when the elephant was young and helpless when he was likely tied to the rope. Back then he learned — was conditioned— to believe that he was too weak to break free and he eventually grew to accept his fate. As years passed and he got older and stronger, he eventually became physically strong enough to free himself. But in his mind, he was still the small, helpless, weak little elephant held in place and unable to escape his bonds. He's really not in physical bondage anymore; he's actually in mental and emotional bondage. He doesn't know his personal power and therefore meekly stays in place, doing whatever he's told to do and putting up with whatever life brings his way. This situation is called *learned helplessness*.

Learned helplessness is when an animal (or a human being) has been conditioned to become passive and helpless; to feel like they have no control over their life circumstances. Research has shown that animals and humans that have been subjected to uncontrollable events or mistreatment without the possibility of escape will eventually stop trying to avoid the situation. In fact they learn to simply accept the negative situation — they learn to become helpless. Even when they're presented with an opportunity to escape, their learned helplessness prevents them from taking any positive action. Both the amygdala and hippocampus have been shown to be involved in the acquisition of learned helplessness.

Like many forms of conditioning, we can even acquire our learned helplessness by indirect conditioning. That means that we don't even have to be subjected to uncontrollable events or situations ourselves to become helpless in our outlook; we can simply have observed someone else, like a family member or close friend, experiencing an uncontrollable experience and learned to become helpless ourselves. As you learned in Chapter Two, this direct and indirect conditioning has significantly impacted your view about yourself and your ability to control your life outcomes. Fear is the puny rope of conditioning that's holding you stuck in place to a life that's restrictive and keeping you from the freedom to pursue a life of power and control.

From the day we were born, when we were young and helpless, our conditioning began. We were helpless to do anything except to merely accept the conditioning of our brain and the emotions that built up in our subconscious mind. This is when we formed our impression of the world and our place in the world. This is when we were programmed by our physical and social environment and came to believe certain things about ourselves. This is when our relationship with Fear began; well before we were emotionally able to develop any conscious self-awareness. This is when we began to form our self-image and, based on our experiences, interpret our self-image in a negative or positive light. If we grew to see ourselves in a negative light, unable to control what happens to us, we aren't likely to take any steps towards making things better for ourselves.

Let me give you an example. Have you ever worn a pair of sunglasses or eyeglasses and come in from the cool outside air into a heated room only to find that your eye glasses have fogged up and you can't see a thing? Living in fear is like looking at yourself and your life circumstances through that pair of foggy eye glasses. When you live in fear you have a fear filled, biased perspective of yourself, the people in your environment, and the situations you may find yourself in. You can't see yourself — your image — or your world clearly. Because you can't see clearly, you feel helpless to take any action. You don't take any steps forward but remain stuck in place. After all, if you try to move around in life with foggy eye glasses on, you're likely to bump into things, trip or fall.

FEAR FACT #27: Living with fear is like wearing a pair of foggy eye glasses. Because you can't see yourself or your world clearly, you feel helpless to take any action.

Fear keeps those foggy eye glasses on you as a way to distort your self-image and use it against you. He reinforces your previous conditioning by causing you to interpret things in your life as unavoidable or unchangeable. He makes you see yourself as unable to change yourself or your circumstances. He makes you think things like "Things will never change" or "I can't do anything right" or "I'm not smart enough" or "I'll fail if I try so why even bother". The more you repeat these negative thoughts to yourself, the more Fear increases his hold over you by driving your warped self-image deep into your subconscious mind and wiring your brain so that your fight-or-flight switch set to "ON" for much of the time. This has profound effects on your mental health (i.e., fear can lead to increased stress, depression and anxiety) and can lead to poorer physical health as well as we discussed earlier.

FEAR FACT #28: Fear makes you feel that you can do nothing to change the situation you're in or your life outcomes. In reality, you already have all the power you need to make any change you like.

Learned helplessness can also have a lot of influence over your decision-making strategies. This is because your learned helplessness over-rides your ability to think rationally. Not only does it reduce the functioning in your prefrontal cortex, but also churns up negative, self-defeating emotions in your subconscious mind that are easily pulled up as self-defeating thoughts in your conscious mind. These thoughts and emotions then work together to influence your behaviors, and as a consequence, your life outcomes. For example, whenever you hear stories about someone who has been a victim of prolonged domestic abuse but has stayed with their partner, learned helplessness is usually one of the contributing factors. It's because of learned helplessness that the abused person fails to see any way out of their negative situation. They feel helpless to do anything else but to remain in the very situation that's causing them to feel fearful. This is an example of Fear's foggy eyeglasses at work.

Are you like that elephant; held in place to a personal or professional life that makes you feel helpless or is holding you back from going after your dreams? Are you looking out towards your forest of freedom but find yourself unable to take a step forward? Remember: when Fear takes hold of your brain and your subconscious mind, he conditions you and makes you believe that you're helpless. This is a false belief but it's what holds you in place, much like the adult elephant held in place by a puny rope. Fear makes you feel that your self-imposed limitations are real. He hides from you the fact that he's the only thing standing in the way between you and your freedom to live a successful and fearless life. By making your fear responses automatic through learned helplessness and limiting beliefs, Fear keeps you mindlessly reacting to life's stressors with fear rather than a sense of personal control.

Some of the questions you might want to ask include:
1. What are some examples of mindless behavior in my personal and professional day-to-day life?
2. How well do I pay attention to my thoughts, feelings and behaviors?
3. How might my mindlessness, my learned helplessness or my limiting beliefs, be keeping me in a state of fear?
4. How might my automatic fear response to stressors be affecting my thoughts, feelings and behaviors without me even knowing it?
5. What things or situations in my past may have led to my mindless, automatic response to stressors?

6. How can I begin to start paying attention to the choices I make with respect to my reaction to the stressors in my life?

7. What are some of the things in my life that could be looked at differently if I took off my foggy Fear eye glasses?

For me, learned helplessness is a very personal experience. I spent most of my childhood and early adult life living in a state of learned helplessness. Like most people, learned helplessness came primarily from my childhood conditioning where, for my generation and in my culture of origin, children didn't have much freedom to exert control over their lives. Like most authoritarian parental households, my childhood and adolescence was an environment where obedience and strict discipline was the order of the day. My parents' parental style emphasized submission to parental rules and regulations with generally little or no reason given for those rules and regulations. I was a child who craved the emotional parent-child connections that I often saw in the homes of some of my friends and on the family television shows of my childhood (like the Brady Bunch). I wanted so much to be like "those people" but learned to accept that, as a child, I didn't have any power to initiate the changes I wanted. And so, I withdrew into myself and spent much of my time reading and finding connections with the characters in my books.

As a consequence of not being able to exert much control over my life from an early age, I learned that life was something that largely happened to me (i.e., life by default) and not something that I could influence in order to meet my own needs and desires (i.e., life by design). Although I did well academically and socially, I was significantly delayed in achieving any sense of autonomy (i.e., freedom to be independent and self-directed). In fact, I was frustrated, depressed and angry for much of my early years. My experience is not unique. Research shows that children raised in an authoritarian home environment are obedient and proficient, but rank lower in happiness, self-esteem and positive self-conceptions (i.e., the mental image that someone has of themselves) than children raised in less-restrictive families.

That sense of learned helplessness shadowed my personal relationships and even my first marriage where I remained tied to a situation that negatively affected my mental and physical health for much longer than I should have. I put up with things that I knew and felt was causing me emotional harm but my automatic, conditioned, mindless response was to stay put; to remain tied to the situation by the puny rope of my self-imposed limitations. It was only when I began to actively and consciously overcome my childhood conditioning and my own negative self-conditioning that I was able to develop a more healthy and positive self-concept. It was only then that I realized that I was no longer the elephant tied to the ground by a puny rope; I was free to wander off into the forest of freedom to take personal control of my own life.

After I took off my foggy eye glasses and increased my self-awareness, I was able to overcome my dysfunctional relationship with Fear and see that, as an adult, I was at that point the only one standing in my way. The only string tying my foot to a stick in the grass and preventing me from running toward the forest of freedom was me; no one else was holding me back from getting the life of my dreams but me. Being conscious and self-aware allowed me to see that I did indeed have choices about the way I could live my life. My early childhood conditioning didn't matter in the long run. It was how I chose to recondition and rewire my own brain and mind, to change my thoughts, feelings and behaviors that really mattered.

So, let that be a source of encouragement to you. Before you start worrying about all the childhood conditioning and self-conditioning that has wired your brain for fear, and all the negative, fearful emotions that you've stored in your subconscious mind that can never be erased, know this fact: *you can control your conscious mind and therefore take control of the information you put into your brain and the emotions around it stored in your subconscious mind.*

So, even if something triggers a stress-response, like fear, you have a *choice* as to what happens next. Remember, your conscious mind is where you have the ability to accept or reject any idea or thought that happens as you interact with your external systems and encounter potential fear triggers in your day-to-day life. As such, you don't have to mindlessly and automatically react with fear when faced with current stressors or when you remember fearful experiences from your past. You can use your conscious mind to re-frame all the emotional memories you've stored up in your subconscious mind so that they no longer influence your thoughts, feelings and decision-making in a negative, self-defeating and fearFULL way.

Remember, your conscious mind is the computer monitor and your subconscious mind is your hard drive. You decide which programs you want to call up to the forefront from among all the installed programs on your hard drive. You choose whether or not you'll continue to let your dysfunctional relationship with Fear continue to put up barriers between you and the successful and fearLESS life you want to live. It all starts with using the power of your conscious mind to reprogram your old conditioning so that you create new neural pathways in your brain and establish new paradigms in your subconscious mind.

Chapter Seven
Moving Beyond Our Fear Limits:
The Power of Choice

"We are not animals. We are not a product of what has happened to us
in our past. We have the power of choice."
Stephen Covey

"The way life treats you is a merciless mirror image of
your attitude toward life."
Anonymous

"Destiny is no matter of chance. It is a matter of choice. It is not a thing
to be waited for, it is a thing to be achieved."
William Jennings Bryan

Our perceived limits, as you now know, and an apparent lack
of choice, are illusions caused by fear. We all have the freedom
of choice; and *choices start with a decision.* You need to decide
that Fear won't be calling the shots in your life anymore. You
need to decide that you want to, and will, rewire your internal
systems so that they no longer automatically obey Fear's
commands. You need to decide that it's time for a change in your
systems; that you want to make them more functional and work
for you instead of against you.

Habitual patterns of responses such as fear, as you now
know, cause neural networks in our brain to be wired together in
such a way as to make fearful responses easier to access and
activate. When we have a fear reaction to a stressor, our
amygdala triggers the fight-or-flight response and works with our
hippocampus to establish and reinforce existing habitual fearful
response patterns.

Our Mind-Brain-Body System

Brain   <===>   Body

Mind

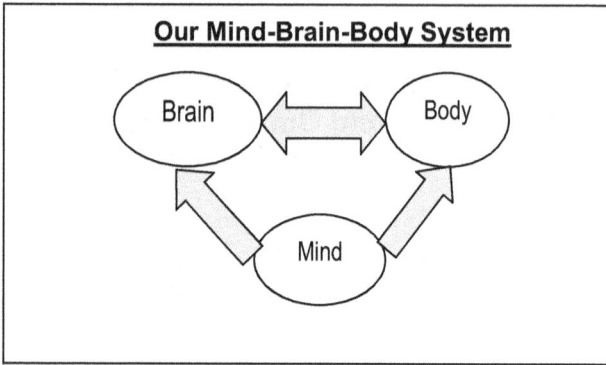

But these habits are also wired into our self-conception and paradigms in our subconscious mind. Our brain gets the information about how to interpret stressors and what to do about them from our subconscious mind which has remembered every single time we've been faced with a stressor in our entire life and how we've responded. Our subconscious mind is where our idea of ourselves as strong and in control or weak and powerless lie. As we've seen, sometimes our mind sends fear signals directly to our body even before our brain has even become consciously aware of what's causing us to feel fearful.

It's clear then that our mind runs the show, not our brain. Our mind, particularly our subconscious mind, is in control of all our internal systems including our brain and body systems. Our mind tells our brain what to do and our brain relays this information to our body. So, in essence, the emotional wiring in our subconscious mind is even more important than the mental neural wiring in our brain. It directs our brain to interpret things as stressful and often amplifies our brain's conditioned fear-response to things because of the emotions linked to our habitual fear response. Making clear choices and recognizing the consequences of those choices are not possible when we're in a dysfunctional relationship with Fear because he controls our mind.

Let's take an example. Let's imagine that someone experiences a stress trigger (like a child running out from between parked cars while he's driving through a neighborhood) and his amygdala automatically activates a fight-or-flight response and he has a fear reaction to the stressor. What happens next is not inevitable. The driver has a choice about how he'll let that stressor impact his behavior and his view of himself as a good or bad driver. He can use his conscious mind to pick and choose his thoughts and inform how he lets that experience affect his feelings about himself. Here are two scenarios with completely different results:

Scenario A FearFULL Outcome	Scenario B FearLESS Outcome
1. A child darts out from between parked cars while a man is driving in a residential neighborhood.	1. A child darts out from between parked cars while a man is driving in a residential neighborhood.
2. His amygdala fires up and his fight-or-flight response causes him to take action (slam on the breaks to prevent his car from hitting the child).	2. His amygdala fires up and his fight-or-flight response causes him to take action (slam on the breaks to prevent his car from hitting the child).
3. He immediately feels himself shaking and his stomach is clenched. He is experiencing a fear response.	3. He immediately feels himself shaking and his stomach is clenched. He is experiencing a fear response,.
4. He pulls over to the side of the road and starts to replay the terrifying event in his mind.	4. He pulls over to the side of the road and starts to replay the terrifying event in his mind.
5. As he replays the event in his mind he begins to re-live the fearful experience all over again	5. But he's mindful of the power of his thoughts. He knows that re-living negative emotions, like

(wiring the memory into his hippocampus and conditioning his subconscious mind for fear).	fear, will only wire it deep into his hippocampus and condition his subconscious mind for fear.
6. He thinks about how many near-misses he's had over the years he's been driving and begins to question whether he may not be a good driver.	6. He thinks about this near-miss and the other near-misses he may have over the years he's been driving and notes that he cannot control the actions of others, just his own actions.
7. He 's completely mindless to the fact that his control of the car helped him to avoid hitting the child as proof of his good driving, but instead begins to perceive all parked cars as a stress trigger; as having the potential for having someone dart out from between them.	7. He makes a conscious decision to continue to be a vigilant and focused driver, on guard for any unexpected actions on the part of other drivers or pedestrians. He also acknowledges that he was in full control demonstrated by his ability to avoid hitting the child.
8. Each time he drives he's a nervous wreck and spends more energy looking at the parked cars than he does keeping his eyes on the road. He becomes a distracted driver and experiences an increase in near-misses.	8. Each time he drives he makes a conscious decision to remain a calm and focused driver. He remains a competent driver and is able to take corrective action when other drivers or pedestrians present a threat.
9. These experiences reinforce his fears and solidify his self-perception as a bad driver in his subconscious mind.	9. These experiences reinforce his feelings of control and solidify his self-perception as a good driver in his subconscious mind.
10. He stops driving because he let his fearful thoughts and beliefs, wire his brain and subconscious mind for fear.	10. He continues to drive because he did not let the negative experience wire his brain and subconscious mind for fear.

As you can see from the scenarios in the table, there were two different outcomes largely as a function of the initial fear reaction when the child ran out from between the two parked cars. In Scenario A, the driver let the fearful experience invade his thoughts and change his view about himself. In Scenario B, the driver, even though he went through the exact same fearful experience as the driver in Scenario A, *consciously chose to take control of his thoughts* and thereby prevent a downward spiral of having that experience get wired into his hippocampus and change his perception of himself in his subconscious mind. He made sure that the information he put into his subconscious mind, by his own conscious effort, was consistent with how he wanted to see himself and how he wanted to live his life.

FEAR FACT #29: Fear is a choice. It is a choice of where you choose to focus your attention and how you choose to interpret the things, situations and people in your environment.

How and where you choose to focus your attention and thoughts is the key to changing your subconscious mind, and hence, your brain. You can indeed use your mind to create awareness of your body, brain and mind and harness their individual powers in order to create the changes you want in your life. This includes the elimination of the fears that are preventing you from moving toward the successful life that you want. The foundation of all this change — from moving from fearFULL to fearLESS lies in the power of your mind; particularly the way you use your conscious mind to influence your subconscious mind and integrate and control all three of your internal systems. In this way, you'll be able to dump fear from your life and begin a new functional relationship with Power. *Your power lies in your choices.*

One of the more enlightening times that I was presented with a choice as to whether or not I was going to let Fear affect my life happened when I was a second-year PhD student. I was a teaching assistant in a course on mental health for third-year undergraduate students, and was responsible for creating and delivering tutorial sessions based on the coursework, marking papers and exams, and holding office hours to assist students in their progress through the course. I excelled in that role and delighted in helping students overcome their learning barriers. I loved teaching and seeing students reach their "Aha!" moments as they grasped new concepts and achieved a sense of mastery over the oftentimes difficult material.

One day the professor came to me told me that he was going to be away for two week's holiday and that he wanted me to teach two of his classes. I was simultaneously fearful and exited. I was excited that he had enough faith in me to teach his class of 250 second-year university students (whom I'd been teaching in small hour-long tutorial sessions of 50 students and not as a large group) but also fearful at the thought of preparing my own lectures for the first time and holding the attention of all those 19-22 year-olds for the two-hour lecture. I was confident about my knowledge of the material — after all, I was an A+ graduate student and knew the material inside out and had been successfully delivering tutorial sessions for some time. However, I had only stood in front of the entire class on previous occasions to proctor exams or to make short announcements. This time I would be expected to prepare entire lectures from scratch and to make the material I presented salient because what I taught would appear on their mid-term and final exams.

I decided to see view this request as an opportunity rather than a challenge; as something to be anticipated with positivity rather than something to be dreaded and feared. I made the conscious decision to take hold of any fear that I was experiencing at the anticipation of presenting the lecture and re-frame the challenge of presenting a lecture as an opportunity to achieve mastery over my fear and over this new experience. I knew that if I allowed Fear to creep into my thinking about the upcoming lectures that I'd be doomed to a self-fulfilling prophesy of failure. So I began thinking "success" and "power" in my mind and with my feelings.

As I prepared the lectures and anticipated my performance, I became very mindful of any fear that would pop into my mind. Each time I experienced a fear trigger (e.g., when students or professors passed me in the halls and reminded me that I was going to be giving the lectures while the professor was away — like I needed to be reminded!) I made a conscious decision to re-direct my attention with positive visualizations (like seeing myself successfully delivering the lectures) and think about what an amazing opportunity it was for me.

With that mental and emotional preparation, and having done the work to create compelling lectures, I walked into the lecture room of 250 students as a seasoned professor in my mind. I had dressed more formally than usual, and the tone of my voice and my body language left no room for confusion as to who was in charge for the next two hours and what my expectations were for their behavior. I had previously decided that there was no way that I would appear fearful or nervous in front of the class. A lecture hall full of young students would quickly become unmanageable if I didn't control the situation right from the very start.

But not only did I set expectations for them (and myself), I also told them how fortunate they were to be learning the material — that the material wasn't just an academic exercise but knowledge that they could apply in their real lives. I wanted to motivate them to learn not just based on external pressures (i.e., to get a good mark on their exams) but because it would impact them internally (i.e., make them more aware of how these concepts were influencing their life).

And you know what happened? The lecture went off without a hitch. In fact it went better than I'd even imagined it would. The students listened attentively and came back promptly from their 10-minute break halfway through the lecture. Even though I had felt a bit of nervousness at the start as I watched the lecture hall fill up with students, all the nervousness went away after the first few minutes. That's all the time it took for me to feel as powerful and in control as I'd visualized while I was preparing the lectures.

As I mentioned, in dysfunctional relationships, one partner has more power and control over the other. Because I was in control of my emotions and didn't let Fear get power over me and dictate how I should feel and behave, the students reacted to me in such a way as to reinforce my feelings of power and control (remember, your internal systems interact with and reinforce your external systems). They paid attention, took notes and didn't leave their seats until they were dismissed. Many even came to see me after the lecture excited to tell me that I'd made the material easy to understand and had used examples that made the concepts more clear to them than the scientific articles (which were their required reading) did. The same thing was repeated the following week after my second lecture.

When the professor returned from his vacation, he approached me and asked me "What happened? They're all buzzing about what an amazing job you did." Furthermore, when the exam results came in, the professor was shocked to find that the students had performed better on the questions pertaining to the lectures I gave than to the other lectures he gave during the term. He wanted to know my secret. I simply told him that I made the lectures not just informative, but also made them relevant by using examples that related to the students; their age group and their life experience. I approached the lecture wanting to teach but more importantly, I had wanted the students to learn.

My own experience of the lectures and the positive feedback I received was confirmation about the power of the mind — the power of internal systems to impact external systems. Had I given in to my initial fear reaction when told that I was expected to give two lectures, the situation would have been completely different. Although I would have had the same brain, and the same intellectual capacity to write and deliver the lectures, my mind would have made me a weak and ineffective presenter. This in turn would have made it more difficult for the students to learn and master the material and perform well on their exams.

Not only did this experience help me wire my brain for success in lecturing, it also wired my subconscious mind to be fearless in other areas of life. Did you know that whenever you have a "win" in one area of life that it wires you for "wins" in other areas of your life? That's because the "win" generalizes or gets transferred from one situation to another (just like computer software programs and files can get transferred from one computer to another). As well, the emotional "win" in your subconscious mind helps to wire the mental "win" in your brain.

This is what I teach my clients who are intimidated by something they have to do. Whether it's anticipation of a job interview; presenting before a Board of Directors; presenting in front of their class; confronting their partner about some dysfunction in their relationship; or facing other fear barriers, I teach them that if they purposefully choose to wire their subconscious mind to think and act powerful and in control, that their brain and body will follow suit. I teach them that, by making the attempt to overcome their fear barriers, they'll eventually experience "wins" and that with each "win" they'll be programming their brain and subconscious mind for more "wins". Eventually they come to realize that the only limits that they had were those of their own perceived limitations.

Limitations are Mind Over Matter

But I don't want you to think that I'm not aware of reality; that I'm saying that all limits are in our imagination. I'm not saying that at all. What I am saying is *the degree to which we see our circumstances as presenting limits to our success is subject to interpretation.* If for example, someone is imprisoned, then that person has real concrete and metal limits as to how far they can go and how they can behave without consequences. But not all people in jail see the same limits; while some accept the prisoner label and begin to have negative views of themself, some anticipate what they'll do when they're paroled and take courses and educate themselves so that they can be a better version of themselves on release. While the environment is the same for both people, the belief systems and reactions are quite different and so are the life outcomes.

Let's take Nelson Mandela as an example. While imprisoned for over 27 years under South Africa's apartheid system, he didn't let the harsh physical limitations of his circumstances dictate how he felt or what he thought. Even while in jail, he kept his mind on the future and wrote manuscripts and motivated thousands of people, and eventually the world. He always expected that something better would come and had a large vision for his future, despite his treatment and confinement. When he was released he went on to help change South Africa's racially divided constitution, won a Nobel Peace Prize and became the first democratically elected Black president of that country.

How different Nelson Mandela, South Africa and the world would be had he not been determined to not let the 27 years of harsh physical limitations he faced define him. Several years ago I had the honor of being in the audience when Nelson Mandela accepted an honorary doctorate from one of the universities in my city. Hearing his story about how he survived that experience with his self-esteem and personal power intact serves as a permanent reminder to me about the power of the mind over limitations; whether those limitations are perceived or real.

Another one of my heroes who demonstrate that limitations are a function of mind over matter is Mary Kay Ash, the founder of Mary Kay cosmetics. She came from humble beginnings and after a divorce and hitting the glass ceiling by being denied promotions at work in favor of men she'd trained, she went to work for herself. Soon after she started her company her new husband and business partner died of a heart attack but she persevered. Her company grew to be among the top companies in America as she pioneered the field of cosmetics.

She also won numerous awards from the business community for being one of the top female entrepreneurs in the world and became a best-selling author of three books. She left a legacy of self-determination (based on her mother's habit of telling her "You can do it Mary Kay") and a mandate to strive for equality in the workforce. She serves as an example for men and women that persistence, hard work and self-determination can overcome structural barriers to success.

The mental health literature refers to the concepts of *fatalism and instrumentalism* to describe differences in people's outlook on life. Fatalists generally believe that they have no personal power to do anything other than what they're currently doing, and think that future events, good or bad, are inevitable and that there's nothing that can be done to change things. They tend to leave everything to destiny and resign themselves to having life unfold for them rather than directing it in deliberate, conscious ways. They tend to live their life by default.

Instrumentalists, on the other hand, are full of intention in their thoughts and their actions; they make things happen. They are instrumental in directing their lives towards achievement of their goals. They make an effort and take personal responsibility for both their successes and their failures. Instrumentalists have more optimism and hope about the future and are less likely than fatalists to have mental health problems such as depression and anxiety. They tend to live a life of their own design.

In general, people's thoughts about their ability to control their outcomes are a result of internal factors or external factors. This is commonly referred to in the mental health literature as one's *locus (or location) of control*. A main difference between instrumentals and fatalists is where they place control. Instrumentalists believe that they're the source of control (i.e., internal locus of control) and fatalists believe that things outside themselves like other people, luck, or fate is the source of the control (i.e., external locus of control). Because of this difference in outlook, instrumentalists are more likely to be self-aware and mindful of changing conditions that they can use to achieve their goals while fatalists are less likely to see opportunities when they arise. Research shows that people with an internal locus of control are less likely to be depressed and anxious than those with an external locus of control.

Because instrumentalists act on opportunities while fatalists tend not to act on opportunities (either because they don't see them or don't think that their actions will make a difference) instrumentalists get more positive feedback and reinforcement for trying. That is, sometimes when they try, they experience "wins" and that makes them feel that their efforts will be rewarded. For the fatalists that don't try, they never get to find out if their efforts will be rewarded; they never get to experience "wins" due to their own efforts. These two perspectives have entirely different consequences for someone's ability to overcome fear barriers.

Locus of Control	
External (Fatalist)	**Internal (Instrumentalist)**
• I'll get the promotion if I'm lucky.	• I'll get the promotion if I demonstrate competence and a desire to succeed.
• I failed the test because the professor dislikes me and is harder on me than other students.	• I failed the test because I didn't understand the material clearly and so performed poorly.
• Most people with money got it because of lucky breaks.	• Most people with money worked hard for it.
• I tried to succeed twice before and failed. So I guess that fate is against me and there's no point in trying again.	• I tried to succeed twice before and experienced setbacks. I'm going to use them as learning experiences and try again.
• Life is a game of chance. It's the luck of the draw.	• Life is what you make of it.

When faced with a stressor that causes them to feel fear, fatalists will tend to fall back on dysfunctional thoughts and behaviors and avoid the stressor (e.g., not ever asking the boss for the raise that was promised to them) while instrumentalists might also first experience a fear response, but set their mind to moving past the initial uncomfortable emotional and physical response to the stressor. They may, for example, look for the right time, when their boss is in a good mood or has just complimented them on a job well done, to remind her of her promise of a raise.

Fear tries very hard to make fatalists of us all. He knows that having an external locus of control where we feel that we have no control over our life outcomes, is a form of stress, and as you now know, stress exposure activates our fight-or-flight response. Having a fatalistic outlook has caused us to have perceived limitations and feel like we have no control over our thoughts, feelings or the circumstances in our life. When we have an external locus of control and react with fear to life circumstances it means that Fear has wired our brain to see limitations even when none exists. He's also programmed our subconscious mind to see ourselves as having no control over our life outcomes. It's our dysfunctional relationship with Fear that keeps us from trying to adopt a more instrumental outlook.

> **FEAR FACT #30**: Living in fear is a choice of orientation. Are you a fatalist (believing that things that happen to you are beyond your personal control) or an instrumentalist (believing that you can change your life by your own personal efforts and determination)?

In the driving example scenario that I used earlier, Person A would be considered to be a fatalist while Person B would be considered to be an instrumentalist. Person A let the negative stressor he experienced put limits on his thinking about his ability to control things that could happen while he was driving. Person B, on the other hand, although he experienced the same negative stressor, didn't entertain having limits on his ability to control his outcomes. The choice that they each made changed their driving outcomes and also changed their lives.

Fear makes us think that our limitations will always stop us from achieving our goals. As I ask my clients who are fatalists in their outlook: "How do you know for sure what'll happen if you try? If you don't ever try, how do you know whether or not you can succeed?" I also teach them the importance of trying so that they can achieve a sense of mastery. Research has shown, for example, that successes give people a sense of mastery or a sense of personal control over their environment. With their new sense of mastery, they're more likely to take chances and try again in the future. They'll be less likely to let Fear get in their way.

You may have heard the phrase "Seeing is believing." Well, to a great extent, what you see is what you already believe. If you believe that there are limits placed on you, then you'll see limits, even when no limits exist. You're seeing your life though the lens of your limiting beliefs based on your prior conditioning and expectations. You're seeing your life through foggy Fear eye glasses.

Fatalism to Instrumentalism Chart

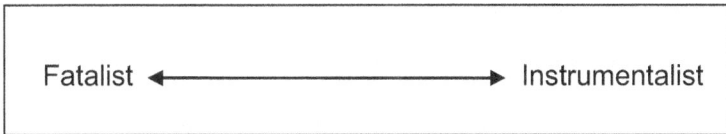

Fatalist ⬅——————————➡ Instrumentalist

Where would you place yourself on the chart above? Are you closer to the Fatalist end of the continuum or the Instrumentalist end? Do you tend to have the same orientation in all aspects of your life (e.g., in personal relationships, in professional relationships, your health, physical exercise, diet, your appearance, etc.) or do you sometimes switch from one orientation to the other depending on the circumstances? Using this chart can help you begin to see how your dysfunctional relationship with Fear may be clouding your perspective on various aspects of your life.

Keep this chart in mind whenever you're faced with decisions, when you're reflecting on certain aspects of your life, or when dealing with something or someone that's causing you to feel fearful. When you look at the chart, ask yourself the following questions:

1. What am I thinking about when making this decision or looking at my life circumstances?
2. Are my thoughts, feelings and actions coming from a fatalist or instrumental perspective?
3. If they're coming from a fatalist perspective, how can I nudge them along the continuum and move towards being more instrumental?

Put this chart somewhere you can easily see it and each day ask yourself: "Am I thinking, feeling and doing things that move me towards being more instrumental in my life?"

Limitations and Personal Control

In order to feel that your actions will have an effect on your desired life outcomes — in order to move from fatalism to instrumentalism and overcome your fears — you need to have a sense of personal control in your life.

	Instrumentalist	Fatalist
Internal locus of control	FearLESS	Not possible
External locus of control	Not possible	FearFULL

As the chart above shows, you can't have a sense of personal control and be a fatalist at the same time. In fact, the way to become fearLESS is to be an instrumentalist with an internal locus of control. Fatalists (with an external locus of control) tend to be fearFULL because they don't see that they can make the changes necessary to change their life for the better.

While you're in an ongoing dysfunctional relationship with Fear, he keeps you in a state of learned helplessness and feeds you limiting beliefs about your ability to take control of your own life. In order for you to break free of his powerful hold over you, you'll need to begin to *take personal responsibility* for your thoughts, emotions and actions rather than seeing your life from his perspective.

Up to this point in your life you've been blindly conditioned by internal and external systems that have caused you to be fearful. This conditioning of your brain and subconscious mind has led you to expect that, for the most part, your efforts to overcome your fears will make no difference to your end results. Most people who are struggling with fears have an external locus of control and tend to be fatalistic in thinking that their fear will always get the best of them and keep them from moving on towards the successful life that they want.

Although we developed our sense of control early in our childhood, our exposure to external stressors throughout our life has also impacted our sense of personal control and our ability to deal effectively with and overcome our fears. In particular, exposure to chronic stress can gradually erode a person's sense of personal control more than exposure to acute stressors. For example, people may have had a sense of personal control when they first begin a new job, but over months or years of being passed over for promotions despite being qualified, working hard and making contributions to the company, some may develop a sense of fatalism in that area of their life. This sense of fatalism reinforces their ongoing dysfunctional relationship with Fear and serves as a source of chronic stress that gradually erodes their perception of personal control over the things that happen to them. In the end, their fear becomes a source of chronic stress for them just like their unsatisfying job is a source of chronic stress.

Like all people, the choices you've made in your life and will ever make are based on your sense of self. Your sense of self is the lens through which you view the world and your perception about how much control you have over your physical and social environment. Your sense of self impacts your decision-making because it taps into your beliefs about what you're capable or not capable of achieving. Fear has greatly impacted your sense of self by wiring your subconscious mind for fear. He has led you to adopt paradigms (i.e., your habitual way of thinking, feeling and behaving) that have placed limits on all your internal systems.

But now you know that you have a choice. You can choose to take control and reclaim your personal power from Fear. The way you come to feel that you have a sense of personal control is to first believe that you do; it starts with your thoughts. Perceived control (which is the belief that we do have control over our lives) has the power to create a positive impact on our mental health, particularly our sense of well-being. In many ways, the perception of personal control and choices can be even more important than the reality of having control — it helps us to battle the learned helplessness and limiting beliefs that Fear has caused us to adopt. So, how do we begin to make good choices when we've been conditioned by our environment and by Fear to make poor choices?

How Thoughts Lead to Results

One of the lessons that I found to be most valuable to me during my PhD statistics courses and while studying for my comprehensive exams in quantitative methodology was the power of causal models to explain complex things. A causal model is one where direct effects, indirect effects and reciprocal effects (or feedback loops) work together to predict an outcome. Scientists use causal models to determine the relative influence of each specific influence to an overall outcome.

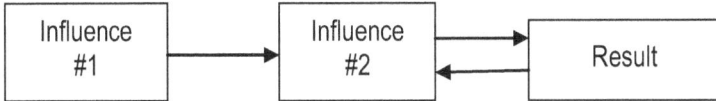

```
┌──────────┐      ┌──────────┐      ┌──────────┐
│ Influence│─────▶│ Influence│─────▶│          │
│   #1     │      │   #2     │◀─────│  Result  │
└──────────┘      └──────────┘      └──────────┘
```

For example, let's say that a researcher has the idea that certain things, such as someone's childhood conditioning (Influence #1), has an effect on their habitual thought patterns (Influence #2) which in turn affects their results or life outcomes (i.e., their overall mental health status like whether they're clinically depressed or not). Their state of mental health then feeds back into their habitual thought patterns which influence their state of mental health in an endless feedback loop.

By breaking down the results into its component parts, social scientists are able to see how life outcomes (like fear learning) comes about, and what factors or influences count the most in predicting the outcome. Because I'm a social scientist by formal training, and see the usefulness of this type of analysis to explain social phenomenon and factors contributing to overall mental health, I tend to touch briefly on the topic of causal modeling in my approach to life transformation.

Although most of my clients moan and groan when I tell them "I'm going to talk to you a bit about statistical methodology for a few minutes", they quickly come to see the importance of breaking down the results they're getting in their life according to how they think, feel and act. In particular, they come to realize the domino effect that having negative fearful thoughts will have on their ability to achieve the results they want to in life. Sometimes it's only when concepts are put in a diagram or in a graph that people can see things clearly. To some, that's when things begin to "click" and to make the most sense. That's because some people are more visual than others in the way they learn and retain information. So, below is a diagram that I've created to use with my clients and in my workshops.

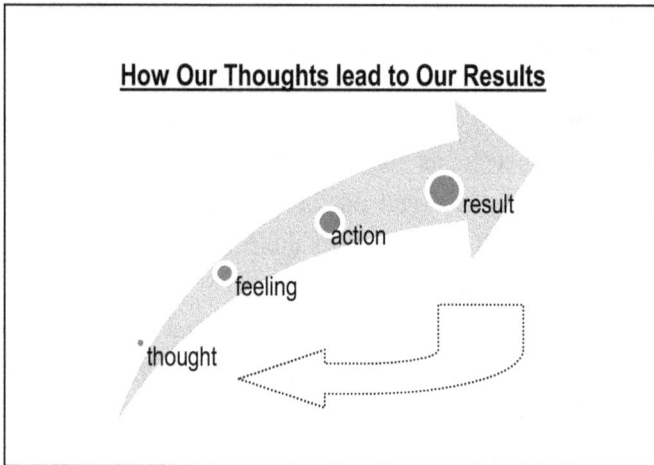

How Our Thoughts lead to Our Results

result

action

feeling

thought

The diagram begins with the first influence (a thought). The thought then leads to a second influence (a feeling). The feeling in turn leads to a third influence (an action) which ultimate leads to the result or outcome. You can see from the diagram that the thought has a direct influence on the feeling, and the feeling has a direct influence on the action (or lack of action) that someone may take. That action or inaction then has a direct effect on the result that the person gets in life. You can also see that the size of the arrow gets larger and larger as we move from thoughts to results. That's my way of showing that even the smallest thought (negative or positive) can have huge effects on life results. The results that the person gets then feeds back and informs their thoughts, which then informs their feelings and behaviors, and the cycle continues.

So, for example, in the case of someone who has a dysfunctional relationship with Fear, they've been conditioned to think primarily in negative and fearful ways. As they think about the thing that they fear, they begin to feel sensations of fear. Once they feel the sensations of fear, their body responds; they generally do something to avoid the situation (the flight option in the fight-or-flight response). Since every action leads to a result, they get the results that come with avoiding the situation. When they get those results, the information feeds back into their thoughts which feed back into their feelings and behaviors and so on.

Let's get more specific. Let's say that Darren is afraid of confronting his wife about some aspect of her behavior that he finds troubling. Specifically, he doesn't like the belittling way she speaks to him in front of their children because he believes that it reduces their respect for him as a parent. But Darren has been conditioned to avoid conflict. When he was a child, his parents continually argued in front of him and his sister and it made him feel fearful that they would get a divorce. So he was always the peacemaker, trying everything he could to patch things up between his parents so that his fear of divorce would go away.

When Darren grew up and got married, he carried with him a fear of divorce as well as his conditioned response to be a peacemaker whenever conflicts aroused in his relationship. Whenever he and his wife experienced conflict in their marriage, his fear of divorce pops into his thoughts. This fear makes him feel nervous and anxious and so he tries to reduce these feelings by avoiding any conflict with his wife; by letting her get her way in all things. But giving up all control in his marriage has costs; it contributes to his wife's irritation with him and her perception of him as a weak and ineffective partner and parent. Because of this, she continues to treat him in a belittling way which only reinforces Darren's poor self-image and fear that she'll eventually ask for a divorce. He lives with the chronic stress of a strained marriage and the fear that the marriage will eventually dissolve. Moreover, he lives with the constant emotional baggage of a poor self-image and a sense of powerlessness over his ability to control his own life.

We see from this example how Darren's thoughts have led to specific outcomes. Darren's thoughts led to certain fearful feelings which led him to behave in specific ways. His behaviors, in turn, led to a certain outcome. The outcome then fed back in a feedback loop and influenced Darren's thoughts. In this way, Darren's thoughts became self-fulfilling prophesies; they led to fearful outcomes.

But Darren can choose to think, feel and act differently any time he so chooses. He can make the conscious decision that he will not let his parents' volatile relationship influence and potentially ruin his own marriage. He can consciously choose to override his old conditioning and stop the negative emotions that arise in his subconscious mind and influence his thoughts.

For example, let's say that Darren decided to think differently. Let's say that he began to think that if he finally told his wife how he felt about her behavior and the impact it was having on the children that she'd be open to listening to him. As he thinks about how he might frame it so that it's not challenging to her but something that she could see as good for the family, he begins to feel less fearful about approaching her. When he finally does approach her he finds that she is indeed receptive to what he has to say and does change her behavior. Moreover, the fact that Darren has finally stood up for himself has won him a new found respect with his wife who'd been waiting all along for him to be more assertive in the relationship. Darren's fear of divorce is greatly reduced and his negative fearful thoughts are all but gone.

Like Darren, the negative fearful thoughts that you have greatly influence the results you get in life. If you continue to have a dysfunctional relationship with Fear, you'll never be able to confront the source of your fears and will never be able to overcome them. Your fearful thoughts will keep leading to fearful outcomes as you continue to generate a self-fulfilling prophesy of fearful thoughts, feelings and actions. If you decide that you can overcome your fears then you'll be motivated to adopt new thoughts, feeling and actions, and begin to live a life of your own design. But if you don't make that decision, you'll just retain your fearful pattern, miss opportunities that come your way, and end up living a life of default rather than the successful life that you deserve.

FEAR FACT #31: Your fearful thoughts lead to fearful feelings that lead to fearful actions. The end result is that your life outcomes reflect your fearful thoughts, feelings and actions.

Whenever you feel that you're responding with fear to a stressor, before you take any action, you might want to refer to the previous "How Our Thoughts lead to Our Results" diagram and ask yourself the following questions:

1. What am I thinking right now?
2. What am I feeling right now?
3. What do I want to do about the way I'm thinking and feeling? What specific action or actions do I want to take?

4. Is what I'm thinking of doing going to help me overcome my fear or does it just allow me to avoid it or even make my fear worse?

5. If I truly want to overcome my fear, not just keep avoiding it, what do I need to do differently, right now?

The goal of asking yourself these questions is to focus attention away from your automatic fight-or-flight response (the amygdala hijack) and give the logical part of your brain and your conscious mind a chance to provide you with rational alternatives. The first two questions will allow you to figure out your thoughts and emotional response to the stressor, the third question will helps to bring your intention about your behavioral response to your conscious awareness (rather than just automatically emotionally responding with fear), and the forth question will help you to determine whether or not the response you're considering is in line with your intentions. The fifth question will give you a chance to think about alternate ways of responding to the stressor so that you can stay on the path to overcoming your fears.

If you ask yourself these questions each time you're faced with a stressor you'll be better able to see over time whether any patterns emerge and how your automatic fear response might be getting in your way of moving from fearFULL to fearLESS. Like Darren, in order to overcome your habitual fear responses, you need to make a choice about your dysfunctional relationship with Fear. You need to decide whether you intend to continue to do what you're doing and keep getting the same disappointing results, or whether you intend to make a change in your internal systems in order to overcome your fear and find your personal Power.

Overcoming your fear habit really boils down to a conscious decision to change and make better choices in your thoughts, feelings and actions. *It does just boil down to two options: Fear or Power.* But what is personal power all about and how do you get it? Let's move on to Chapter Eight to discuss how to transform yourself from fearFULL to powerFULL.

Chapter Eight
What is Power Anyway?

"A great power ... is under your control ... greater than of all your fears and superstitions combined. It is the power to take possession of your own mind and direct it to whatever ends you may desire."
Andrew Carnegie

"Our deepest fear is not that we are inadequate. Our deepest fear is that we are powerful beyond measure."
Marianne Williamson

"Before we acquire great power we must acquire wisdom to use it well."
Ralph Waldo Emerson

What does it mean to have power? There are many definitions of power including the ability to impose one's will on others and force them to do things against their will or their own interests. This kind of power is directed outwards; towards controlling or dominating others in order to get one's way or to elevate oneself. This is a negative use of power.

It always saddens me when someone in a position of power wields their power like a hammer over the heads of others. People who use their power negatively are always quick to let you know what power they have and that they're in charge. They're quick to find fault in others but rarely accept any personal responsibility when they themselves stumble or fail. These people often have legitimate authority (i.e., the power to control others in a particular situation like the workforce or a school room because of their role or status) but they abuse that power.

In my previous careers in academia and corporate life, before I founded Wired2Succeed and was able to choose who I worked with, I had the opportunity to work for, and often worked with, people who abused the power of their position. I noticed that their behavior made work life a source of chronic stress for the people over whom they had authority. They appeared to be singularly focused on holding on to and increasing their own power rather than being invested in helping others to become empowered.

The kind of power that'll help you to overcome your fears doesn't strive to have power over others. The type of power that is true power and the only one that will move you from fearFULL to fearLESS is directed inward. This type of power is *personal power* or *empowerment*. This power focuses on your positive emotional, mental, and spiritual features and strives to master the self, not others. This kind of power focuses on imposing your will towards achieving control over your internal systems — mind, brain and body — and translating that will into reality in order to shape your destiny. This kind of power strives to achieve your desired quality of life without violating the rights of others.

You should be aware that this definition of personal power also embodies the element of change — our ability to change our internal systems and our external systems so that they align with our goals for our personal and professional success. When we have this type of power, we have the ability to control and take personal responsibility for ourselves and the choices that we make. We can make changes in our life and can react appropriately to life changes that come our way. We have control over our thoughts, feelings and actions and don't let situations or other people control how we think, feel or behave. We have the peace of mind that we'll be able to handle any emotional or physical stressor that we're faced with. This type of power allows us to be self-determined, confident and competent.

FEAR FACT #32: Personal power is all about being able to take control and responsibility for your thoughts, feelings and actions; to use your internal systems to drive you towards the achievement of your goals without violating the rights of others.

Achieving a sense of personal power impacts our mind, brain and body systems. When we're truly empowered, we have high self-esteem, a high sense of mastery and will want to use our gifts to help not only ourselves, but others as well. Truly empowered people don't do things to impress others; they do what they believe is right and what's consistent with their sense of self and their core values. Empowered people give easily, laugh easily, love easily and forgive easily. They're flexible in their approach to people and situations, and are open, optimistic and positive about what they have to offer and what life has in store for them.

Research shows that people who have a sense of personal power and believe that they can control their life outcomes have a number of positive attributes. For example, they have a strong sense of self; define and set their own goals; are better able to problem-solve and cope with stressors; are more likely to take risks; are self-reliant; have a clear understanding of the impact of their decisions on their quality of life; are resilient and better able to bounce back from negative experiences or setbacks; are less likely to suffer from mental health problems such as depression or anxiety; and, are also less likely to suffer from many physical health problems.

While we're in a dysfunctional relationship with Fear our sense of personal power is seriously compromised. In this relationship, Fear is in control; he's the one with the power. He has used his power in a negative way towards us and has conditioned and manipulated us to think, feel and act the way he wants us to. Over time, the relationship became increasingly unhealthy and eroded our sense of self, our self-esteem, and our self-awareness. Fear put foggy eye glasses on us and made us see limits where there are none. At times the relationship may have even impacted our physical health since Fear keeps us in fight-or-flight mode for most of the time. Now we look at ourselves and our life and find ourselves being fearful in situations where we'd like to have control; where we need to have control and power. Fear has gotten into our systems, and now our systems have become inefficient and ineffective in moving us towards the successful and fearless life that we want.

But it didn't start out like that. At first the relationship seemed perfectly fine and Fear seemed to be a great partner for us. Fear made us aware of, and responsive to, real physical threats (like enabling us to slam on the break to prevent us from hitting the car in front of us). But things slowly took a turn for the worse and eventually Fear didn't just want to have power over our response to physical stressors; he wanted power over our response to emotional or psychological stressors as well. He used his power in a negative way and eventually he even had us responding to emotional stressors that were largely a product of our imagination; based on our perception or over-exaggeration of a threat in our social environment caused by a fear-based paradigm.

As you read in Chapter Three, dysfunctional relationships are characterized by an imbalance of power — one partner dominates the emotional climate of the relationship while the other consciously or unconsciously gives up power to remain in the relationship. However, functional relationships have more balanced power dynamics and one partner doesn't dominate the other in any way. They each bring their own strengths to the table and the relationship is better for it. Functional and healthy relationships bring joy and happiness to the people involved and each partner finds personal satisfaction in helping and seeing the other mature, grow and reach their goals. Emotional needs are largely met within the relationship itself because both parties make sure to do things that are in the best interest of the relationship. Moreover, healthy relationships are based on reality. Each person sees the other as real; with all their strengths and weaknesses.

In our dysfunctional relationship with Fear, he doesn't want us to see things as real at all. He wants to keep foggy eye glasses on us where we live in a world full of biased self-perceptions including low self-esteem, learned helplessness, an external locus of control, and a lack of self-awareness. In that way Fear can prevent us from growing and maturing and overcoming our fears and anxieties. Our relationship with Fear is a relationship based on dishonesty; he's dishonest with us, and as a result, we've grown to become dishonest with ourselves.

As long as you remain in a dysfunctional relationship with Fear you'll keep depending on him and remain helpless to assert yourself. You'll keep giving up your personal power and Fear will continue to get his own way in how you think, feel and behave. Since Fear will never change, don't you think that it's time to move on? Don't you think that it's time to dump him and find a better life partner for yourself?

That better life partner is already waiting for you. That better life partner is Power. He's been waiting for you to notice him and all that he has to offer you. You just haven't noticed him as yet because you have your foggy fear eye glasses on. But Power has noticed you and he wants you to know that with him you'll finally find the life-affirming relationship that will lead you to the successful life you've been longing for. With him you'll be able to overcome the fear barriers that stand in between you and the personal and professional life of your dreams. Your relationship with Fear was dysfunctional, but your relationship with personal Power will always remain functional and healthy.

When you're in a functional and healthy relationship you'll feel:

- Confident
- Secure
- Empowered
- Fulfilled
- Appreciated
- Respected
- Encouraged
- Liked/Loved
- Trusted
- Cared for
- Nurtured and emotionally supported
- Free to express your true self

If you compare these signs with the signs of a dysfunctional relationship in Chapter Three, you'll see a significant difference. While Fear took away your rights, Power freely gives you rights, including your right to:

- Be yourself
- Be happy
- Determine your own priorities
- Be proactive rather than reactive
- Change and grow as you become more self-aware

- Ask for and go after what you want in life
- To not be responsible for the happiness of others. Their happiness is their responsibility
- To be honest with yourself and expect honesty from others
- Say no to requests that don't line up with your values
- Treat others well and expect to be treated well in return
- Have healthy personal and professional relationships

You developed your close, intimate relationship with Fear over time by spending lots of time with him. In the same way, your relationship with Power will increase in intimacy and closeness the more time you spend with him. As you grow closer to Power you'll begin to feel more self-confident as he encourages you to pursue your dreams. Rather than forcing his own thoughts, feelings or habitual behavior patterns on you like Fear did, Power will encourage you to become more self-aware. He'll help you to determine what it is you truly want and he'll give you the confidence and courage to go after it. Rather than defining you, he'll allow you to finally define yourself, free from the conditioning and programming of others. Rather than limiting you, he'll encourage you to overcome your learned helplessness and limiting beliefs. Where fear would say to you "No you can't", Power will say "Yes you can".

In this way, Power will gently push and challenge you to think, feel and behave in a way that gets you closer to realizing your full potential. He'll boost your self-esteem and show you that you're capable of making the changes you need to harness the power of your internal systems towards the achievement of your goals. Perhaps even more important, when you enter into a relationship with Power you usually discover a meaning and purpose for your life — your worthy ideal — because you're no longer looking through the foggy eye glasses that Fear had put on you. You can see yourself and your life clearly and make conscious decisions about how you'll use your personal power to enrich not only your own life, but the lives of your loved ones and others.

Moving on from Fear to Power

Just like in real life, it can be a bit difficult to determine if we should stay in a relationship and try to make it work or if we should end it before it gets any worse. But one thing is for sure, if one partner in the relationship is abusive in any way, including emotional abuse; it's time to take some form of action. One of the best ways to spur us into action is to ask ourselves some serious questions about the relationship. For example, in terms of our relationship with Fear, we might ask ourselves:

1. Do I like myself less than I normally do when I spend time with Fear?
2. Does Fear respect my right to make my own life decisions without having his controlling influence overshadow them?
3. Is he happy and encouraging about my ambitions and dreams or does he get in the way or even try to sabotage my attempts at success?
4. Do I sometimes feel powerless in my relationship with Fear?
5. Will my personal and professional life be as successful as I'd like them to be if I stay in this relationship with Fear?

At this point in reading *Dump Your Fear!* I trust that you've taken the time to ask yourself the questions posed along the way. Combined with these questions you've just asked yourself, you'll be better equipped to reflect on your relationship with Fear and increase your self-awareness. Self-awareness, as you now know, is an essential part of growing in your consciousness and will help you align your thoughts, feelings and actions with your goal of overcoming your fears and growing in your own personal power. Without self-awareness, there's a significant risk that you won't overcome the fearFULL thoughts, feelings and actions that are barriers in your path to the successful future of your dreams.

Part of being self-aware also means that you need to reflect on how and why the unhealthy relationship developed in the first place. In the case of your dysfunctional relationship with Fear, you need to reflect on how your past conditioning and your habitual ways of thinking, feeling and behaving have contributed to the maintenance of the relationship. Many people, for example, go from one dysfunctional relationship to the next because they didn't take the time, or make the effort, to become consciously aware how their thoughts, feelings and actions contributed to the dysfunction in the relationship. Remember, a social relationship, by definition, involves more than one person so each person makes a contribution to the relationship and has to assume some responsibility for how it functions.

People who don't take the time to reflect, and take on some of the responsibility for the dysfunction in the relationship (no matter how small) tend to repeat the same pattern. Because of this, they end up meeting and dating the same type of people over and over again and wonder why they can't find Mr. or Mrs. Right. Or they quit a job in haste and go on to find work that they eventually find to be just as unfulfilling and unrewarding as the one they'd left. Or they make friends with new people only to find out that they get used and disrespected just like they did in previous friendships.

In other words, they keep getting into dysfunctional relationships with people and circumstances and keep repeating the same pattern because they keep taking their faulty programming with them into these new relationships. They never take the time to consciously reprogram themselves; to replace their old dysfunctional patterns with new positive ones. They keep experiencing the same life lessons over and over again, never quite grasping what it is they're supposed to learn from their experiences.

During our first session, many of my clients bemoan the fact that they keep getting into the same painful life situations over and over again. They're in a vicious cycle and don't realize their role in perpetuating the cycle of disappointment in their personal and/or professional life. In many ways, they think, feel and act exactly like I did before I became self-aware; before I stepped back and examined my own role in the cycle.

For example, one of the things I did immediately after my divorce was to take some time to get to know myself. I went through a time of self-imposed social isolation by reducing my exposure to outside influences including other people and various media (e.g., television, magazines, radio, etc.). Not only did I need to take some "alone time" to reflect on how I'd let fear and my past conditioning keep me in a dysfunctional relationship, I also needed to figure out who I really was at my core, and what I wanted out of life. I had to learn to become more self-aware. Like most people in a dysfunctional relationship, my needs and desires had been seriously compromised because I'd given up my personal power to maintain the relationship. After the divorce, I had the opportunity to explore my own needs and aspirations and develop my internal systems to reflect those needs and aspirations.

In order to grow in self-awareness I had to take personal responsibility for having given up my power even though it had occurred slowly over time and had occurred on a mainly unconscious level. I had to face my own role in the dysfunction in order to take control of my thoughts, feelings and actions. When it occurred to me that my power hadn't been taken away from me but that I'd actually given it up, that realization freed me. I had made the choice (even though it was largely an unconscious one) to give up my personal power in the marriage. So, with that knowledge, I could make the choice to never let that happen again. I was in control. I had the power of choice. I had made poor choices in the past but could decide to not make those same choices in the future. I wasn't powerless after all; I had power all along. It was just that I'd had Fear's foggy eye glasses on and couldn't see that I had choices.

Now free to think, feel and act in my own best interest, I was free to discover my own power not only in personal relationships but in all aspects of my life. As you increase your self-awareness, and evaluate your own thoughts, feelings and actions, you'll be able to make the changes necessary to take control of your thoughts, feelings and actions as well.

FEAR FACT #33: Increasing your self-awareness is important to overcoming your fears and is a necessary step before you can begin a lifelong relationship with Power.

A chief component of personal power in the psychological literature involves the concept of *self-efficacy*. Similar to instrumentalism, self-efficacy is the belief in our own ability to accomplish whatever goals we set out to accomplish; that we can do whatever we set our mind to. Our sense of self-efficacy, instrumentalism and internal locus of control are all tied to our belief system (our paradigms) held deep in our subconscious mind. All play a crucial role in our beliefs about our own abilities.

Because of this, a sense of self-efficacy is necessary for us to begin to feel that we have power and control over our own thoughts, feelings and actions — that we can change not only our internal systems, but our external systems as well. People with high self-efficacy think, feel and act differently than those with low self-efficacy because having self-efficacy causes them to believe and *act on their beliefs* that they can create a life of their own design rather than living a life of default. When they act on their positive thoughts and beliefs, their external environment provides them with results that reinforce their beliefs.

Research shows that people who think they can control their own lives have many positive attributes. They're more powerful; have higher self-esteem; are better able to set goals and motivate themselves to go after and produce the results they desire; are prepared to meet challenges; develop healthy personal and professional relationships; and have better mental and physical health. In fact, research also shows that people can even begin to change their lives and overcome habitual dysfunctional behavior patterns without a lot of professional counseling if they learn to develop their self-efficacy and self-regulate their thoughts, feelings and behaviors.

Although your sense of self-efficacy has been influenced by your childhood conditioning and your self-conditioning, you can consciously choose to re-condition and reprogram yourself at any time. You can consciously choose to move from fearFULL to powerFULL. Remember, the way to begin to change your lifelong conditioning starts with over-riding the programming in your brain and subconscious mind; by replacing the malicious fearful code that Fear put in your systems with your own code for fearless, powerful thoughts, feelings and actions.

Because the way to get to your subconscious mind is through your conscious thoughts, you'll need to start thinking and feeling that you're capable of change. You need to start to believe that you can indeed move from fearFULL to powerFULL. You need to believe before you can take any meaningful action. *It's the feeling, the perception that you'll be able to make the change from fearFULL to powerFULL that gives you the power to act.* And feelings begin with thoughts. Remember, both your brain and your subconscious mind make no distinction between the things in your imagination and what's real. If you imagine that you have power and control, your brain and subconscious mind will follow suit and give you the courage you need to exercise your power and control in real life. If you believe that you're fearLESS, then your feelings and actions will have to follow suit.

Your positive thoughts and beliefs will urge you to try to do something new, to take calculated risks, and to not give up at the first setback or when you run into resistance from other people. Your positive thoughts and beliefs, held in your subconscious mind and funneled through your brain and conscious mind, are what will give you your power. Having a sense of self-efficacy puts you on the path to your personal power.

Preparing for Change

But you need to be prepared to make a change in your life. You need to be prepared to do the work that it will take to move you from fearFULL to powerFULL. You need to make a choice about whether or not you'll continue your dysfunctional relationship with Fear or will dump him for a healthy and functional relationship with Power. After reading to this point, you now know that your relationship with Fear is unhealthy and has harmed your brain, mind and body. But like so many of us who've been in dysfunctional relationships, the fear of change keeps us rooted in the very dysfunction that's causing us harm. At this point you might want to ask yourself:

1. What specifically do I want to change about the fearFULL way I think, feel and behave?
2. Why do I want to change at this point in my life?
3. What has prevented me from making this change in the past?
4. In what specific ways will my life and the lives of my loved ones be better if I make the decision now to change from fearFULL and powerFULL?

Based on your answers to these questions you can determine whether you're emotionally and mentally prepared to make the change. Where would you place yourself on this "Stages of Change" chart?

Stages of Change	
Pre-contemplation	You're not really considering making a change in your life (in your thoughts, feelings or actions) at this point. This is mainly due to denial or a lack of awareness about the consequences of your thoughts, feelings and actions on your life outcomes.
Contemplation	You've become more aware of the benefits of making a change; of moving from fearFULL to powerFULL. But at this point, you're still struggling with the costs of changing versus the benefits.

Preparation	You've decided that the benefits of changing outweigh the costs. You begin to make small changes to prepare yourself to overcome your fears. For example, you might read a book about overcoming your fears in order to get information about what you will need to do to make the change.
Action	You take direct action towards overcoming your fears and gaining your personal power; you act on your new thoughts and feelings and the things you have learned during the Preparation stage. You keep motivated and reinforced by using proven strategies and surround yourself with supportive and positive people.
Maintenance	You have achieved the ability to think, feel and act differently by conscious choice. You have moved from fearFULL to powerFULL. Your self-awareness keeps you alert to the triggers that might cause fearful thoughts, feelings or actions and you continually use the powers of your subconscious mind to affirm yourself as a fearless person.

Where you fall on this chart is a reflection of your readiness to move on from Fear to Power. How ready are you? Are you in the Pre-contemplation or Contemplation stage? Are you still holding on to doubt and indecision about trying to make a change? Or are you in the Preparation stage and have made a decision that enough is enough and that it's time to take control of your life? Are you ready to take that first small step towards overcoming your fear barriers?

If you haven't arrived at the Preparation stage as yet, allow me to share something with you: did you know that a fear of change is actually a fear of failure? It's not changing that you fear; it's the fear of trying to change and not being successful at it. So like most people you avoid the thing you fear. You procrastinate. But making no choice actually is making a choice. Like the saying goes "if you fail to choose, you choose to fail". Like all of us, you don't escape the consequences of not making a choice. Making no choice leads to a life of default rather than a life of your own design. So you do need to choose, and you need to choose now.

You want to overcome your fears and the things getting in the way of your personal and professional success don't you? You want to feel and be powerFULL, right? Well, you can't feel fearFULL and powerFULL at the same time; neither can you be fearLESS and powerLESS at the same time. Like the chart below shows, fear and power can't occupy the same space — they're logically and emotionally inconsistent with each other.

Which Will You Choose?		
	PowerFULL	**PowerLESS**
FearLESS	**Live your life by your own design**	Not possible
FearFULL	Not possible	**Live your life by default**

So, you need to make a choice. How do you want to think, feel and act for the rest of your life? In order for any of us to feel powerful we must turn away from our fears. When we give in to our fears, we give up our personal power. And when we give up our personal power, we give up our right to live our lives by our own design. You have a right and a responsibility to yourself and to those you care about to live your life to your full potential. Make the decision to choose Power over Fear.

But there's one important thing that you need to know before you start to make the transition from fearFULL to powerFULL. Your relationship with Fear was entered into unconsciously through your early childhood conditioning and the conditioning you continued to receive as you grew up programmed your brain and subconscious mind for fear. *Your relationship with Power*, on the other hand, *must be entered into consciously.* You must consciously re-direct your thoughts, feelings and actions in the direction that you want to go so that your subconscious mind will receive the message and get to work creating the life you've imagined.

When you make the conscious decision to choose Power over Fear, you've taken a tremendous first step down the path towards personal fulfillment. Once you dump Fear and move on from that relationship, you'll finally be able to see all the conditioning, limiting beliefs, learned helplessness and other negative influences that he has had in your life. Once free from Fear, you'll be able to finally and completely embrace a relationship with Power. And unlike your relationship with Fear where he wanted to control everything (including your thoughts, feelings and actions), Power wants to give you control. Rather than feeling threatened, Power delights in seeing you prosper. He wants to always have a healthy, functional relationship with you; one where you'll feel safe and secure in the knowledge that you can control your own life outcomes.

Chapter Nine
Upgrade Your Mind Systems to Find Your Power

"We cannot solve our problems with the same thinking we used when
we created them."
Albert Einstein

"What lies behind us, and what lies before us, are tiny matters
compared to what lies within us."
Oliver W. Holmes

"Men and women are not prisoners of fate,
but only prisoners of their own minds."
Franklin D. Roosevelt

I trust that, by now, you've come to realize how our
dysfunctional relationship with Fear has caused damage to our
internal systems; how he's caused our brain, mind and body
systems to function well below their optimum level. When our
overall internal system isn't working properly, it needs to be
upgraded to a more effective and efficient system — one that'll
allow us to get the fearLESS, successful life we want and
deserve; a life that will move us from fearFULL to powerFULL.

In evaluating whether or not a system should be upgraded,
we first need to understand the limitations of the current system;
we need to understand the weaknesses in its performance. Over
the last few chapters, we've done just that. We've examined our
brain, mind and body systems and have determined that Fear has
caused damage to our ability to have our life function the way we
want it to. Fear has reduced the overall performance of our
internal systems which has had consequences for the relationship
between our internal and external systems.

Remember, as you learned in Chapter Three, our internal systems (i.e., brain, mind and body) and external systems (i.e., social and physical environment) are interconnected and interact with each other. For example, because our internal systems have been compromised by our dysfunctional relationship with Fear, we haven't been able to control our thoughts, feelings and actions. The end result is that we under-perform in our personal and professional life because our external systems reflect and reinforce the limitations or weaknesses in our internal systems.

When I was managing and training corporate teams for optimal job performance, I often referred to the saying "we are as strong as our weakest link". That was meant to convey to my staff that we were all part of a system; something larger than our individual selves and that our collective strength rested upon our individual strengths. It was also meant to motivate each of them to do their best given that the team's collective performance was contingent on the performance of each and every single one of us; if one member of the team was an underperformer then the collective — the team as a whole — would suffer. In the same way, if your mind is the weakest link (like it is for most people) then your entire internal system is at risk.

But there's good news. Even if your mind is the weakest link in your internal systems, you can change things. You can use your mind to change and upgrade your mind. Specifically, you can use your conscious mind to initiate changes in your subconscious mind which will eventually transform and reprogram your internal systems. As humans we not only have a powerful brain, but we also have an even more powerful mind. It's by using our mind that we can modify the past conditioning that affects our thoughts, feelings, behaviors and our life outcomes. As discussed in Chapter Six, when we become self-aware or mindful of what we're thinking, feeling and doing, we become conscious of the impact of our internal systems on our life outcomes. When we become self-aware and mindful, we bend our genetics and our conditioning to our conscious will.

As you now know, our brain is modified by our experiences and conditioning but so is our mind. The power of neuroplasticity (the ability of the brain to rewire itself) and the power of our mind to reframe our emotions and replace unhealthy paradigms is the key to rewiring our entire life. It's the key to upgrading our internal systems. We aren't stuck with the brain or mind we've been conditioned to have, neither are we stuck with the life we've been living. We have the unique capacity to rewire our brain and willfully redirect our mind to determine how we think, feel and behave. This will allow us to control our life outcomes, and also help us to add value to our life and those of others.

Firefighters provide us with a great example of how our conscious thoughts can overcome our programmed instincts and conditioning. Most people would agree that all human beings have an innate fear of fire. Millions of years ago our ancestors learned that getting too close to fire could lead to physical injury and even death, and so over time our species have become genetically wired to "flee" in the face of fire. It's now an automatic part of our fight-or-flight fear response, like it is in animals. People will instinctually run from a burning building, not into it. However, firefighters have overcome that conditioning and have instead rewired their brains and reprogrammed their minds to be able to run into burning buildings when others are running out. Thanks to their conscious choice to override their genetic programming and early conditioning, they save thousands of people each year.

Remember, your prefrontal cortex is the part of your brain that's responsible for higher-order thinking like reasoning and processing sensory information. When you respond to a stressor, although the fight-or-flight response might be automatically triggered (i.e., the amygdala hijack), you can also use your prefrontal cortex and your conscious mind to change the perception about what you think, and how you feel, about the potential stressor. The emotional component about how you interpret things and situations in your external environment is a function of the information you've put into your subconscious mind. And, *you can re-frame the memories and emotions in your subconscious mind by using the power of your conscious mind to tell your subconscious mind what to do.*

FEAR FACT #34: Your subconscious mind holds the key to re-programming and upgrading your internal systems.

Unlike our conscious mind that is at rest while we sleep, or anesthetized during surgical operations, our subconscious mind is always at work, even while we dream at nights. It takes in everything. Because it takes in everything from our senses it needs our conscious mind to focus it; to tell it which of the millions of memories we should pay attention to. It also tells us how we feel about those memories and how we should react to them. Remember, your subconscious mind is like the hard drive on your computer containing all the programs and software you've ever loaded onto it. Your conscious mind, your computer monitor, displays only the programs and files that you decide you want to work with. It focuses on what you consciously decide to call up and pay attention to. Similarly, what we spend our time thinking about in our conscious mind is what our subconscious mind focuses on and reflects back to our conscious mind, brain and body. In that way, *whatever is impressed in our thoughts must be expressed in our feelings and our actions.*

For example, if you've gone through your day focusing on thoughts about how you're not getting the things you want from your life, how everything seems to be out of control, and how afraid you are that you'll never overcome your fears and limitations then that's all your subconscious mind has to work with. While you sleep, your subconscious mind digs though all the files in your hard drive and plays some back to you in your dreams. Your dreams at night are likely then to be illustrative of the fears you focused on during the day. When you wake in the morning, your conscious thoughts are even more fear-filled than they were the day before and the cycle repeats itself the next night, and so on.

But one of the amazing things about great systems, like our internal systems, is that they're able to change. In fact, one of the most notable elements of a fully functioning and efficient system is that it's responsive to changes in its environment and can make adjustments accordingly. Much like computer operating systems, your internal systems — brain, mind and body — can be upgraded to newer, better, improved versions that function more efficiently and effectively.

A Change of Mind Changes Everything

The way to upgrade your internal systems begins with your mind. It's where you'll focus your energy and gain more control over yourself and your external environment. It's where you'll *Dump Your Fear!* and begin your new relationship with Power. Your mind provides you with the ability to reprogram and upgrade your internal system and end your relationship with Fear.

One of my favorite cartoons as a child was Hanna-Barbera's Scooby Doo. A group of four teenagers and their talking dog Scooby Doo were called the "Mystery Gang" and drove around in their Mystery Machine (a van) solving mysteries. Most times they investigated sightings of ghosts and monsters that were terrorizing a town or a particular building. When they arrived at the location they'd begin to investigate the seeming paranormal activity and would often split up in singles or pairs to look for clues. While they looked for clues, they'd often accidentally come face to face with and be chased by the monster or ghost.

Scooby Doo was afraid of the monsters and ghosts. In fact, he would try to avoid doing anything that would bring him into contact with them. But he was part of the Mystery Gang "system" and had a role to play in the Gang's ability to solve the mystery; they all had to contribute to solving the mystery by looking for clues. It took a lot of prompting and coaxing to get Scooby Doo to change his mind and help the Gang find out where the monster or ghost was lurking. In fact it took a Scooby Snack — a doggy treat —to get him to change his mind.

But, once he changed his mind about helping to solve the mystery he was able to contribute to the Gang's investigations. As he looked for clues, he'd eventually stumble into a solution to the mystery and find that a human villain was behind the entire thing rather than a real ghost or monster. The human villain had used deceit and guile to make it appear that he was a powerful monster or ghost. This had given him the opportunity to cover up his crimes because the people believed the deception and reacted in fear based on their beliefs. Invariably each episode ended with the unmasked villain saying: "And I would have gotten away with it too, if it hadn't been for you meddling kids."

If Scooby Doo hadn't changed his mind and made the conscious choice to confront his fear, the Gang wouldn't have been able to solve the mystery and the villain would've gotten away with his sneaky schemes. The Gang and the townspeople would never have known that there was no real monster or ghost to fear and all their false perceptions would have gone unchallenged. They would have run away in fear and the phony monster or ghost would have gotten what he wanted.

Like Scooby Doo, when we make up our mind to confront our fear, to change our habitual dysfunctional thoughts, feelings and behaviors, we solve the mystery of why our life hasn't been going well for us. We solve the mystery of why we haven't been getting the results we want despite our efforts to do so. And like Scooby Doo, when we change our mind and confront our fear, we eventually find out that the very thing we'd feared isn't as scary or powerful as we'd imagined. In fact, we find out that *we're significantly more powerful than the very thing that we were afraid of.*

The root of our emotional fears is based on a perception in our subconscious mind, not the reality of the situation. Like the monsters and ghosts in each Scooby Doo episode, the things you fear are actually not as scary as they appear to be in your thoughts. In fact, once you end your dysfunctional relationship with Fear, you'll find that he's actually pretty weak and easily controlled. The only way he had power over you is because you gave your power to him. Like most people who use their power in a negative way, Fear is actually very weak. He tried to compensate for his own feelings of powerlessness by gaining power over you, and you let him do it.

Like Scooby Doo, the only way to get over your fear is to make a choice to confront it so that you can take back your personal power. In order to find the strength to do this you have to rely on the fact that you already have what it takes to do so — you have your wonderful mind. You must trust in your innate abilities and realize that you can take control of Fear's hold over you simply by making the conscious choice to do so. Don't let fear scare you away from living the life you've always wanted to live. Your Scooby Snack, your enticement to face and overcome your fears, is the promise of a new life — a new life of empowerment and control over your own destiny.

Mind Power

The way you think about things is 100% effective protection against fear. Although your genetic heritage and your conditioning have had an influence on the person you've become and has played a significant role in the formation of your fears, the largest and most significant impact on your life outcomes *right now* is the choice you make every single day to think, feel and behave in certain ways.

Thoughts and feelings can be referred to as "red herrings" or "canaries in a coal mine"; they tell us about what's going on in our subconscious mind. By paying attention to your thoughts and your feelings, by being more self-aware, you'll start down the path toward making the changes necessary to end your dysfunctional relationship with Fear. Whether your fear is instinctive, conditioned by others, or a learned habitual response to stressors, you can learn to change from fearFULL to powerFULL. Like the firefighters who ignore their instinctive conditioning to avoid fire so that they can confront the flames to save lives, we also can ignore our prior fear conditioning.

Your mind is where you'll make the choice to completely re-frame your memories and re-invent a new you by your conscious efforts to become more self-aware and mindful of the habitual fear responses that have been working against you. These new fearLESS thoughts, feelings and behaviors will become your new habit and replace our old patterns and paradigms. These new paradigms will cause your subconscious mind to function more effectively and efficiently. This will in turn improve the way your entire internal systems function. You'll find that you'll get the life results you want in less time and with less overt effort.

> **FEAR FACT #35**: The results you get in life, your life outcomes, are a result of the actions set in motion by the workings of your conscious and subconscious mind.

Like your brain, your subconscious mind makes no distinction between imagination and reality — if you tell it to think weak and fearful thoughts, then you'll keep feeling and acting weak and fearful in your life. Your system will remain the same. But, if you tell it to think powerful thoughts, then you'll begin to feel and act more powerful in your life. So, the lesson to be learned is that *we must choose our thoughts carefully because they will lead to predictable outcomes*: think fearful become fearful; think powerful become powerful.

Using the power of your mind is how you'll be able to make the good choices you need to overcome your dysfunctional relationship with Fear. Remember, your brain and body has no choice but to do what your subconscious mind tells them to do. And your subconscious mind has no choice but to think what you consciously tell it to think. Regardless of the fact that it's stored everything you've ever experienced, it's your interpretations, and the emotions associated with those interpretations, that are important.

There's absolutely nothing wrong with the quality or design of your internal systems. They've been created to function perfectly for you if you use them correctly. Fear has interfered with your ability to use your mind, brain and body correctly and so your internal systems are failing to work for you; failing to get you the results you desire. Your subconscious mind, when used properly will serve you in productive ways. You'll get overwhelmingly positive results if you make the decision to upgrade your internal system and make conscious attempts to upgrade your thoughts.

Let's take Carla as an example. Carla first came to see me because she'd had a lifelong relationship with Fear. Although she'd progressed to senior management within her company, she secretly suffered from a sense of helplessness about her ability to overcome her past parental conditioning that had predisposed her to a fear of failure and a fear of being judged in a negative way. She'd tried therapy before but it hadn't worked for her and she'd resorted to taking prescribed medications in order to reduce her physiological symptoms (i.e., trembling, sweating, rapid heart rate) whenever she had to make a presentation at work or at a social function. However, recently her job description had evolved to include more visibility in the company which meant that she was required to make frequent speeches to company employees and to her clients. She knew that her fear was going to get in her way of her professional success and sought my help.

Over the period of a few weeks of coaching she was a transformed woman; making impromptu speeches and getting positive feedback from her audience about how calm and poised she looked during her presentations. And she did all this without the aid of medication. How did she do this? She did this by upgrading her internal operating systems, by taking control of her prior conditioning and reprogramming her brain and her subconscious mind. Prior therapy that focused on only one part of her systems had not helped her overcome her fear of public speaking. She'd needed to incorporate my holistic mind-brain-body-spirit approach to transformation in order to overcome her lifelong fear habit.

Like Carla, you too can upgrade your internal systems and stop fear from getting in the way of your success. But you first need to start thinking that you can control what happens to you in order to break Fear's hold over you. You need to begin to believe that you can overcome your fears, be financially successful, have quality romantic, personal, and professional relationships, and whatever else it is you set your mind to. And you need to use a specific proven system like the one I used with Carla and my other clients to help to harness the power of your subconscious mind.

Ultimately your subconscious mind knows how to get you what you want; it holds all the answers you're looking for. It's where you'll find your power. For example, do you remember the strangulation nightmares I mentioned in the Preface of this book? If you recall, I'd been living in a dysfunctional marital relationship for some time but was too fearful to leave; I was stuck in the Contemplation stage in the "Stages of Change".

Near the end of the relationship, I began to have frequent nightmares that someone was standing over me as I slept and attempting to push me back down as I woke and tried to rise from the bed. In these nightmares, the shadowy figure was actually putting his hands around my shoulders and neck to prevent me from rising. He was imposing and menacing and wanted me to stay down. The more I struggled, the more he tried to push me back down and control me. It was only when I continued to struggle and eventually overpower him that I was able to break free of his hold.

These nightmares were terrifying and each time I awoke with my heart pounding and bathed in sweat. Periodically, over the course of my childhood and early adulthood I'd have the occasional nightmare, like anyone else, but they'd never been so real and so consistent in their imagery. But here I was having the same nightmare over and over again. It was only later, after I dissolved the marriage and realized that the nightmares had suddenly stopped, that I clued in to the fact that the answer to my internal stay-or-go debate that had ruled my Contemplation Stage had been in my subconscious mind all along. In fact my nightmares were trying to give me the answer I was seeking.

Those nightmares were an expression of my subconscious mind and were essentially a representation of the impressions and real desires of my conscious mind. My nightmares were telling me that my marriage was strangling me and preventing me from having any power over my own life. It was pushing me down and trying to control me, while I was struggling to rise and get away. But I couldn't understand the message from my subconscious mind while I was awake because I wasn't self-aware and was easily confused by the fearful thoughts in my conscious mind; thoughts about what would happen if I left, how I was going to manage financially, and would I ever find true and lasting love.

Since then I've learned to pay close attention to my subconscious mind, including my dreams. Had I been more self-aware back then, I would've saved myself years of emotional pain and struggle and financial hardship. I wasn't able to make the link between what I was consciously thinking and what was happening in my subconscious mind and missed the obvious signs. It's my fervent desire that you don't waste valuable years of your life like I did living in emotional turmoil and struggle. You need to make sure that you're in touch with the way your mind works; particularly your subconscious mind.

In my undergraduate and graduate studies, I became an expert in psychology and mental health. I studied how conditioning influences the brain and behavior, and how people's emotional health is largely a function of their social environment and their ability to cope effectively with stressors. At that time I believed that this knowledge held the key to unblocking my own personal limitations and would enable me to help others unblock theirs. It was only later that I discovered that this was only a piece of the puzzle.

Although it was an important piece of the puzzle, how our brain works to influence our thoughts, feelings and actions was not the entire picture; a piece of the puzzle was still missing. It was only later, after I explored alternative perspectives and received specialized training about the power of the mind and spirituality, that I discovered that *the mind is the most crucial influence on our life choices and life outcomes*. I learned that the mind was superior to the brain and can actually instruct the brain in terms of our thoughts, feelings and responses to life circumstances.

It was only when I directed my energy and study towards the development of my subconscious mind, not just my brain, that I experienced a seismic shift in my thoughts, feelings and behaviors … and my life outcomes. It was then that I was able to fully heal not only myself, but those who relied on me to help them through their own life transformation.

That lesson however, came at a price for me and the price paid was more than the hundreds of thousands of dollars I spent getting a formal university education and specialized training. The price paid was in the emotional pain and years spent struggling to find out why, despite my academic knowledge, I continued to be unable to manifest the type of life that I wanted and hadn't achieved the level of personal and professional success that I'd dreamed of. Since then I've used my holistic mind-brain-body-spirit system to transform not only myself but countless others. I've overcome my own fear barriers and have helped others to break through their dysfunctional habitual thoughts, feelings and actions to get the lives that they want.

But transformations don't happen overnight. When we attempt to overcome any habit, we have to learn a new one to replace the old one. Similarly, we have to replace our old fear habit with a new power habit. When we first venture to step out into our own personal power, we're trying to do something that we've historically told ourselves and had conditioned our brain and our mind to believe that we couldn't do. Our internal systems will initially rebel and it'll seem like we aren't moving easily in the direction we want to. That's because our brain, mind and body have been programmed to think, feel and behave in habitual predictable ways and will try to go back to the state that they're familiar with.

By moving from a fear habit to a power habit we're adopting a new paradigm and attempting to undo a lifetime of fear conditioning and fear social learning. When we try to reset our subconscious mind to power rather than fear, it's like trying to install a new program on a computer that's been used to running malfunctioning software. This malfunctioning software called Fear has infected our current internal operating systems like a computer virus. What we're trying to do is install a new program; a new system of power to override that virus.

This new power system is incompatible with our existing fear system and at first our internal systems — our brain, mind and body — will give us the message "Error: Incompatible Software" and try to reject the new power system we're trying to install. After all, our internal systems are used to running on fear, not power. This new, strange power system is at odds with the dysfunctional fear programs we've installed over a lifetime of conditioning and self-sabotage.

But don't give up on the first attempt when you get the "Error: Incompatible Software" message. Try again. The new power operating system won't be fully loaded and installed on your very first try. You'll need to reboot your system and restart it several times. Sooner than you might imagine, you'll find that your internal systems will completely accept the new power operating system and override your old dysfunctional fear operating system.

FEAR FACT #36: When you set about to change your fear habit to a power habit, you're adopting a new paradigm and changing lifelong conditioning. Be patient and don't be discouraged by stops-and-starts in the process. You'll succeed in over-riding your old dysfunctional paradigms and fear conditioning quicker than you might think.

Your new power operating system is a permanent installation that can't be overwritten or deleted unless you consciously and deliberately choose to do so. You keep your new power system running clean and virus-free by making sure that you diligently scan for potential threats; by using the "Power Tools" and the information provided in this book to make sure that nothing except positive, affirming, powerful thoughts, feelings and actions enter your internal system from now on.

Every system needs a power source in order for it to function. For example, all the technologies we use (like our computers, phones, televisions, microwaves, etc.) have a power source that provides them with energy. So, what's the power source for our internal system? Well, it's universal energy. That's right, universal energy is the power source for our mind, brain, body ... and spirit. We learn more about universal energy in Chapter Ten.

Chapter Ten
Universal Energy: Your Ultimate Power Source

"Everything is energy and that's all there is to it. Match the frequency of the reality you want and you cannot help but get that reality. There is no other way. This is not philosophy. This is physics."
Albert Einstein

"Things are not happening to you. Things are happening because of you."
Anonymous

"Every choice you make has an end result."
Zig Ziglar

As you now know, we're comprised of internal systems and operate within a world of systems. But did you know that all of creation, the universe itself, is a system? And like all systems, it requires a power source to function? The power source for all systems, including our internal operating systems, is universal energy. Universal energy is the most powerful form of energy there is. It's the vital life blood that runs within and between all things in creation including humans, animals and plants. Universal energy is unlimited; without beginning and without end. It's the key to all power.

Because you're part of creation, you're also connected to universal energy. In fact, you have universal energy flowing through you every second of the day — through your internal systems — although you're likely unaware of it. The only reason why you haven't been able to access this unlimited power source to help you get the successful life that you want is because Fear has been getting in the way of that connection. In essence he's been short-circuiting the connection between you and your power source leaving you weaker and less able to function at your full capability.

The ultimate purpose of universal energy is to be used to grow in empowerment and self-awareness so that you can be the best you that you can be, and in doing so, contribute consciously and meaningfully to the rest of humanity. That's because universal energy not only binds our internal systems together (our brain, mind and body) but it also binds us to the rest of the world, and to creation itself. For that reason, universal energy is often associated with spirit and referred to as spiritual energy. When we tap into our ultimate power source — universal energy — we become conscious of needing to have all our internal systems in alignment and also conscious of wanting to be aligned with the universe. We can't do that when we're in a dysfunctional relationship with Fear because he severely limits our self-awareness as he deflects the focus off of us and puts it on him.

You, and every other human being, are linked to universal energy though your subconscious mind. How does that work, you ask? Well, the simple answer is that everything in the universe is made up of energy; electromagnetic forces and matter. So, not only does universal energy flow through your systems, you yourself are made up of energy. The physical sensations you feel in your body, your thoughts, your emotions and even your paradigms are all energy. Because you're energy, and your thoughts and feelings are energy, you're inextricably linked in to the energy of the universe. When you become truly self-aware, you become conscious of how energy flows through and works within your internal systems and with universal energy to manifest the fearLESS and powerFULL life of your dreams.

Let's perform a little exercise as a demonstration. Rub your palms together briskly for about 30 seconds. When you do that you'll find that you've generated some heat in your palms. Heat, like the heat from the sun, or the heat you use to provide warmth in your home, is energy. Next, move your palms away from each other until they're about an inch (2.5 centimeters) apart. Now bring them together but don't let them touch. Repeat this quickly about 10 times; back and forth, back and forth. You should feel as though your palms are pushing against something spongy; something with a little "give" to it. What you're feeling is your very own energy field.

The energy produced by the emotions in our subconscious mind, and expressed through the energy in our thinking, rational conscious mind and parts of our brain is what's responsible for our ongoing relationship with Fear. In essence, the interaction and energy exchange between our conscious and subconscious mind informs our brain which then causes us to label those feelings and behave in response. The way our brain informs our body, and our body responds with actions are also an energy exchange. The energy in our subconscious mind is connected to universal energy; our unlimited power source. So when we're in a dysfunctional relationship with Fear, this is reflected in the type of energy that our subconscious mind is relaying to the universe.

FEAR FACT #37: Your subconscious mind is what connects you to your unlimited power source which is universal energy.

Did you know that you've probably already had some experience with energy and perhaps didn't realize it? For example, have you ever had an interaction with someone and felt that you were being drained; that you felt worse after being in the presence of that person than before you started the conversation? You couldn't put your finger on it, there was nothing negative or overtly threatening about the conversation, but you left that person feeling a bit disturbed and ill at ease. That disturbance was caused by you absorbing the negative energy from that other person. When you unconsciously absorbed their energy, your internal systems incorporated that negative energy into your energy. That changed your emotions and led to a discomfort in your body and you felt that "ill at ease sensation."

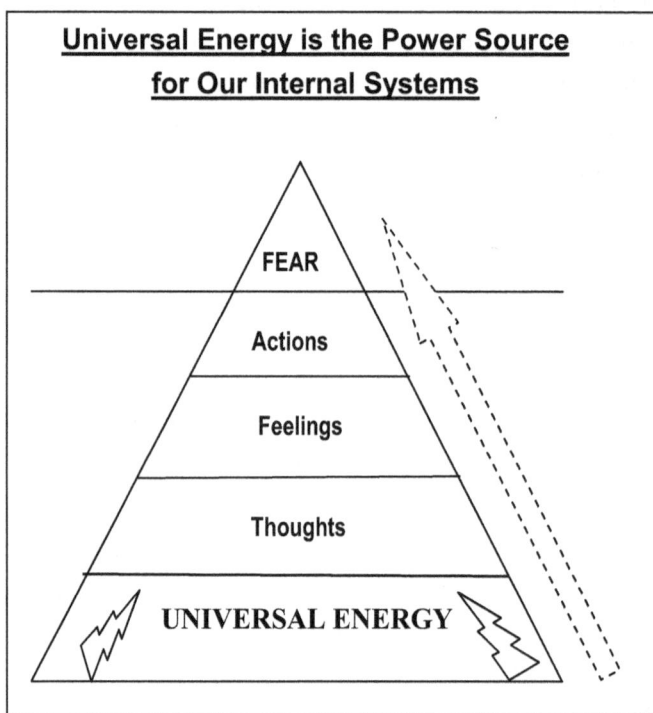

Universal Energy is the Power Source for Our Internal Systems

FEAR

Actions

Feelings

Thoughts

UNIVERSAL ENERGY

Disturbances in your energy field can therefore come from sources outside of you (your external systems) and aren't just due to disturbances in your internal systems (e.g., interactions between your conscious and subconscious mind, and your brain). It's these experiences that occur well below your level of consciousness that can send fight-or-flight signals to your brain (your amygdala), bypassing your conscious mind, and you suddenly experience fear symptoms for no apparent reason. Whenever that happens, your subconscious mind is trying to tell you something.

As you grow in self-awareness and mindfulness, you'll begin to notice when you suddenly feel strange or fearful for no obvious reason and will be better able to determine whether that fear trigger was due to disturbances in your internal systems or due to unconscious energy exchanges with people with negative energy. That's because self-awareness helps you look at yourself objectively (remember, in Chapter Six, I defined self-awareness as the ability to see yourself as a unique object in the world, apart from other people, in terms of your traits, feelings and behaviors). For more information on how to recognize fear triggers, and developing self-awareness and mindfulness, see the "How to take a Fear Trigger Audit", "How to Increase your Self-Awareness" and "How to Achieve Mindfulness" sections in Chapter Twelve.

> **FEAR FACT #38**: It takes a lot more energy to remain in your dysfunctional relationship with Fear than it does to confront him and move on to a healthy lifelong relationship with Power.

Because universal energy is the power source for all your internal systems you need to direct your subconscious mind towards emotions that are consistent with positivity and power. Because everything that is impressed must be expressed, your new thoughts will result in new feelings and actions and new outcomes. Living in fear takes your energy and focus and diverts it into negative thoughts and behaviors that get in your way of taking real control of your life. Living in fear is a major detour off the road to success.

Universal Energy is Neutral but Our Emotions and Thoughts Are Not

Universal energy is neutral. It has no negative or positive value; it just "is". However, much like our personal power, our own personal energy can be negative or positive. Because our own personal energy can be positive or negative, emotions and thoughts, which are a form of energy, can also be positive or negative.

Emotions are a form of energy that, like our blood, flows through every cell in our body. But unlike blood that takes a fluid form, emotion is an electromagnetic energy and runs through our body like an electrical current. When we experience an emotion, like fear, our subconscious mind sends out an electrical current along the neural pathways in our brain and body systems. This electric current stimulates neurons in our brain (for example the neurons in our hippocampus and amygdala) which in turn stimulates neurons in our body and gets it ready for fight-or-flight.

Because energy is always flowing within and around us, we can't stop it or suppress it; *we're always transmitting and receiving energy*. For that reason, we can't just pretend that our dysfunctional relationship with Fear isn't doing real harm to our brain, mind and body. The underlying fear that resides in our subconscious mind is still sending out energy; taxing our body and using up a lot of mental and physical energy that we could otherwise devote to something else; like overcoming our fear and achieving a successful life.

Fear is a form of negative emotional energy that tells you that something is wrong, and like all emotions, is prompting you to do something about it. When you stay in a dysfunctional relationship with Fear, you keep the negative energy flowing throughout your body and building up in your subconscious mind. This has a huge impact on your ability to move forward in life; in fact you can't move forward at all until you deal with your fears. Even if you think you're moving forward without this step, your fears are still affecting you subconsciously and limiting the success you'll be able to achieve.

Because emotions are energy, when we hold habitual fearful beliefs, the energy that's sent to every cell in our body is negative energy. This negative energy is what leads to the deterioration of cells and to physical and emotional issues as the negative energy builds up in our internal systems with nowhere to go. Remember, our automatic fight-flight response compels us to want to do something physical when faced with emotional stressors just as it compels us to do something physical in the face of physical stressors. In the case of a physical threat, when we fight or run away, our emotion of anger or fear and the energy they've generated is expressed (directed outward) and the stress hormones are released and our internal systems get back to a state of homeostasis.

But in the face of most emotional or psychological threats we can't do anything about them and so our emotions can't be expressed outwardly. For example, we can't generally explode with anger and tell off the boss who constantly criticizes our best efforts or the coworker who insists on getting his own way on team projects. As a result, those bottled-up negative emotions are impressed (directed inward) and the stress hormones accumulate in our internal systems.

This buildup of emotional energy is also not good for us — it is negative energy — and can lead us to not only have problems with fear, but to also have problems with anger, depression, guilt, shame and other negative emotions. In that way, the saying "whatever is impressed must be expressed" holds true; whatever thoughts and emotions you have inside of you, in your subconscious mind, must express itself in some way. In the case of response to emotional stressors, that expression is usually in the form of issues with fear and other forms of negative energy.

> **FEAR FACT #39**: Fear is not only a negative emotion but it is also negative energy coursing through your internal systems. This negative energy is what is being sent out into the universe through your subconscious mind.

Our thoughts, like our emotions, are also a form of energy. Our emotional subconscious mind is linked to unlimited universal energy, and receives information about what to focus on from our thinking conscious mind. Because our thoughts form the basis for all our emotions and all our actions, there's possibly no more powerful form of energy than our thoughts. Because our thoughts precede our emotions and actions, they can be considered to be the seeds of our emotions and actions.

Did you know that every seed contains energy in the form of potential? For example, if you hold a seed of a mighty oak tree in your hand; the seed is not the tree but is actually the potential of the tree. If you plant that seed in fertile soil and nurture it, it will grow into its full potential which is a mighty oak tree. That is, the energy contained in the cells of the seed will set about to realize the seed's potential. But if you plant the seed in infertile soil and fail to nurture it, it'll fail to thrive and won't reach its potential because the energy can't fulfill the seed's potential. In both cases, the potential for a mighty oak tree was already there but just in seed form; all you had to do was nourish it.

It's the same with your thoughts. If you nurture a positive thought seed, it'll grow into a positive emotion which will grow into a positive action. The result of you planting and nourishing a positive thought seed will be a mighty positive life outcome. On the other hand, if you fail to nourish the positive thought seed, it will dry up and die. It won't be able to turn into positive emotions, positive actions and positive life outcomes for you. You'll have failed to act on the potential that lay in the energy of your positive thought seed.

One of the most devious ways that Fear blinds us to our own inherent power is by making sure that we think in negative ways and say negative things to ourselves. When we say negative things to ourselves we're actually using the power of words against ourselves. Yes, *words also have energy and power, just like thoughts and emotions do*. Thoughts are actually just words that you speak to yourself; they're your unspoken words. When you engage in negative self-talk by speaking negative words to yourself about yourself, you're actually failing to provide nourishment to any positive thought seeds that you might have.

During my undergraduate studies, I took several courses in psycholinguistics. Psycholinguistics is the study of psychological and neurobiological aspects of language. It was in these classes where I discovered that words not only have a cognitive component, but they also have an emotional component. Through the use of words people are not only able to communicate factual information, but they are also able to communicate emotional information. A person's choice of words, their tone and even their rate of speech has meaning. Sometimes the emotional component of language is even more compelling than what's being communicated factually. In fact, words can be so compelling that they can move people emotionally.

For example, you may have said, or heard someone else say "I was moved by his words" or "Her words moved me". This implies that the words the person used, or how specifically the words were used in terms of their tone and emphasis, caused you or that person to experience a particular emotion or range of emotions. Your subconscious mind registers every single word you say or hear, and based on your paradigms and past conditioning, will assign them a negative or positive meaning. This meaning is then conveyed to your brain which then conveys the information to your body. Research in the field of neuropsychology has shown a close relationship between words and activity in the brain. In particular, there's evidence that negative words stimulate different areas of the brain compared to positive words or neutral words.

As I said before, words have power and energy. Your words spoken out loud or internally (self-talk) can be fear-based and reflect negative energy, or they can be power-based and reflect positive energy. The power of your words, echoed in your self-talk — your thoughts to yourself — has the power to help you overcome your dysfunctional relationship with Fear, or keep you in that relationship with him.

The power of our conscious mind to reprogram the negative paradigms in our subconscious mind lies in the power of the words spoken to ourselves and how we see our place in the world. The words used in our self-talk holds the key to our ability to use our subconscious mind to harness the unlimited power of the universe. That's why it's so important that you don't engage in negative self-talk and say things like "I'm always going be fearFULL" or "I can't control my fears" or "My fears will always get the best of me". Since every thought has an image, the image you're conveying by the words you choose to say to yourself about yourself and your place in the world, paints a vivid picture for your brain and subconscious mind. That's why the things we say to ourselves have such a powerful impact on how we feel and behave.

> **FEAR FACT #40**: FearFULL thoughts (including the words you use in your self-talk) are also negative energy. Negative self-talk will cause all the gears in your internal systems to generate negative energy.

When you repeat fearFULL words to yourself by thinking negatively, you create even more negative neural patterns in your brain and program your subconscious mind (that remembers and believes everything you tell it) to be even more fearFULL. So be conscious and mindful about the words you speak to yourself because words are thoughts, and thoughts lead to feelings and feelings lead to actions, and actions lead to life outcomes. In the words of Ralph Ellison, "If the word has the potency to revive and make us free, it also has the power to blind, imprison, and destroy." Make sure the words you use are powerFULL ones.

In sum, much of the results we get in life depend largely on our thoughts and emotions, specifically whether they're negative or positive. Our thoughts and emotions allow us to be as powerFULL as we want to be; they're the things that define who we are and shape our destiny. Since our thoughts originate in our conscious mind and our emotions originate in our subconscious mind, it's important that our conscious mind and subconscious mind work in harmony with each other.

You've probably heard the term hand-eye coordination which is when someone coordinates their eye movements with their hand movements to achieve an objective (like when a person reaches, grasps and manipulates a knife and fork to take food from their plate and bring it to their mouth in the process of eating a meal). Well, in the case of our conscious and subconscious mind, it's essential to have conscious-subconscious coordination.

You need to make sure that what you want to happen in your life and the fearLESS and powerFULL person you want to become is imprinted in your conscious thoughts and your subconscious feelings. If you fail to do that, the emotional energy in your subconscious mind, since it's linked to the universal power source, will be the predominant energy flowing through your internal systems. If that energy is full of negativity and fear, your life outcomes will reflect this. But if you consciously choose to reprogram and recondition the negative paradigms in your subconscious mind with positive ones (by developing self-awareness an internal locus of control, self-esteem, using positive words, etc), you'll be able to overcome your fears and achieve success. Like the famous quote from the Buddha states, "The mind is everything. What you think you become." In other words, what you think of, you attract to yourself because thoughts lead to feelings, feelings lead to actions, and actions determine your life outcomes.

The Law of Attraction

In order to overcome our dysfunctional relationship with Fear and enter into a relationship with Power, we have to become more self-aware; we have to become more conscious about how our thoughts, feelings and actions have kept this relationship going. Fear isn't just staying in this relationship with us by accident; he's staying in this relationship with us because we keep him in this relationship by constantly giving out and attracting a certain type of energy.

We can get rid of Fear by consciously choosing to change our thoughts. When we make the conscious choice to change our thoughts from fearFULL to powerFULL, from negative to positive, from hopeless to hopeful, our subconscious mind has no choice but to work in conjunction with that new direction. It must set the gears in our internal system in motion towards generating and attracting fearLESS and powerFULL positive energy. In this way, we eventually manifest the very life that initially was only in the emotional realm of our subconscious mind.

The way this works is through the *law of attraction.* In essence, the law states that people attract to themselves what they think about in their conscious mind and the beliefs that are held in their subconscious mind. In other words, people attract to themselves the things they think about when they attach emotion to their thoughts. We attract things to us based on the frequency rate of our personal energy. Specifically, *the energy of the universe responds to the energy and vibrational frequency held in our subconscious mind.* The law of attraction works on universal energy; and like universal energy the law of attraction is neutral, being neither negative nor positive. Just like gravity isn't selective (it pulls everything towards it), the law of attraction isn't selective either. The universe simply returns to us the energy that we send out.

Your energy is what anchors you to the life you're currently living; if you send out positive energy, you receive positive energy back in many forms. If you send out negative energy, you receive negative energy back in many forms. In that way, the law of attraction works like a magnet; you attract to yourself what you consciously think about in your brain and conscious mind, and feel and believe about yourself in your subconscious mind. But since your subconscious mind is linked to universal energy, if there's any inconsistency between what you think and what you feel subconsciously, what you feel wins out because that's what the universe responds to.

You can't see the energy you're generating or attracting to yourself. All you can see are the consequences of that energy in terms of your bodily symptoms, the thoughts of your conscious mind, and the results you're getting in your life.

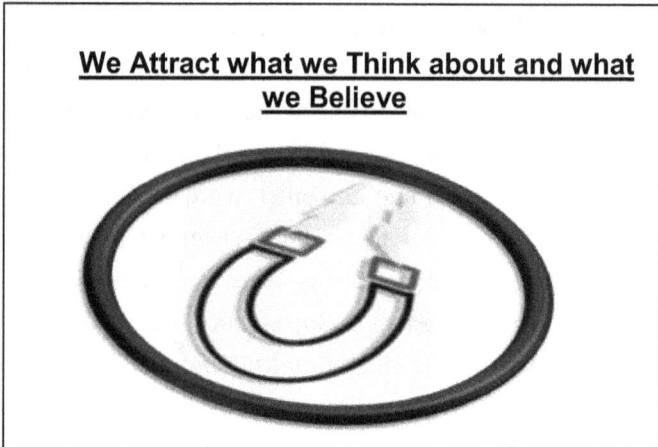

We Attract what we Think about and what we Believe

So many people attract to themselves negative experiences because they subconsciously send out negative energy into the universe, even if they think that they're being positive. So, for example, if you think that you'll meet Mr. or Mrs. Right, but subconsciously really feel that all you'll ever meet is Mr. or Mrs. Wrong, then what you'll attract is what's in your subconscious mind — the universe will ensure that your external environment reflects your expectations and beliefs right back at you. Or, if you subconsciously believe that you'll never get the promotion you deserve, then all your conscious efforts to work hard to get recognition will never manifest in the longed-for promotion because your subconscious mind is sending out negative energy. For this reason, you must develop self-awareness, to ensure that your conscious mind and subconscious mind are properly aligned (for more information on developing self-awareness you can refer to "How to Increase your Self-Awareness" section in

Chapter Twelve). You have to make sure that your beliefs and emotions are aligned with your conscious thoughts and actions.

I'm living proof that the law of attraction, combined with purposeful action, really does work. Before I remarried I was deliberately single for quite a number of years. During that time I had my share of long-term relationships and my share of dates. But I never married any of those men because I didn't feel in my gut that any of them was right for me. No matter how wonderful they were they weren't "the one". But the time came when I grew tired of being single and decided that it was indeed time for me to get married.

At first, I continued to date and remained friends with men who I had no intention of marrying while waiting for Mr. Right to come along. But you know what, he never did come along and I began to wonder why. Then I had an "Aha!" moment. It became clear to me that I hadn't been applying my own transformation system to this particular aspect of my life. My approach to dating was set on "automatic" rather than being a deliberate, mindful, conscious approach. As such, I was sending mixed messages to the universe — the thoughts that I'd generated in my conscious mind about wanting to find "the one" weren't aligned with my emotions or my actions.

So, in order to fix things and align all my internal systems, I had to ensure that my subconscious mind believed what I was consciously telling it and begin to act accordingly. I made a decision to stop dating and devoted my time and energy to friends, family and my work. In order for the law of attraction to give me what I desired, I had to fully devote my mental, emotional and physical energy to what I wanted. I couldn't turn my positive visualizations of a happily ever after life with the man of my dreams into reality while I was actively creating negative energy in my subconscious mind.

I even went one step further. I called up my best friend and announced that I was no longer single and would be getting married the following year and that we should go shopping for a wedding dress. She was incredulous given that I'd ended a relationship just one month earlier. But given my history of achieving the goals that I'd set for myself, she agreed to go shopping with me. I also made my announcement to other close friends and family.

And you know what? The law of attraction worked even quicker than I'd imagined. I found my husband, "the one", the man of my dreams, in record time. My husband jokes that one day he had an unrelenting urge to call me. You see, he and I had been in a relationship for a year but had gone our separate ways about six months earlier, after having ended the relationship on good terms. We had many things in common, wonderful chemistry, and were great friends but were in different stages in terms of our readiness for a committed relationship. But that one day, six months after our break-up, and with both of us having had dated other people, he kept looking at my number on his phone and saying to himself "I have to call her. I need to call her." It's as if something was lit within him. When he told me this after we'd reunited, I smiled and told him that his urge to call me was simply the universe bending to my will. Interestingly, what he experienced occurred within days of my having made the conscious decision to get married.

As is often the case, the universe gave me even more than I'd visualized. He was even more wonderful than before our break-up having grown in his own self-awareness during that time. What had happened was that we were of similar thoughts and energy, and the universe attracted us back to each other even though I wasn't consciously aware that it was him that I had set out to attract. After I announced my engagement and moved to a new, larger house outside the city, a colleague of mine confessed to me that he was amazed by how quickly my vision for my life was coming to fruition and how lucky I was. I told him that I didn't believe in luck but that I believe in the law of attraction and taking purposeful action based on my thoughts and feelings.

That lesson to me is a constant reminder that no matter how developed my level of self-awareness, I, like everyone else, need to make sure that I apply it to *all* aspects of my life. The law of attraction, combined with deliberate action to make sure that your internal systems are aligned, will work in all areas of your life. Like me, you'll find that it gets easier to attract situations and people to come into your life at the exact time that you need them to. When you incorporate the power of the universe into your personal strategies to overcome your fears, you'll be able to increase your own personal power exponentially.

Our Life and Universal Energy

The common denominator for our internal systems is energy — energy generated by our thoughts, feelings and actions. Our subconscious mind has connected with universal energy and has manifested in our life in various forms.

We don't have to be religious or even spiritual to tap into the power of the universe. Universal energy is neutral; neither positive nor negative. It's whether our thoughts, feelings and actions are negative or positive, fearful or powerful, that sets the laws of attraction in motion to give us either positive life outcomes or negative life outcomes. What we get out of life therefore is the sum total of the things and situations we've unconsciously or consciously attracted to ourselves by the way we habitually think, feel and behave as depicted in the table on the following page.

Life is the Sum of the Choices we've made about what to Think, how to Feel, and what to Do		
	FearFULL	**PowerFULL**
Brain choices (Think)	I can't	I can
	I should	I choose
	I might	I will
	I hope	I know
	A problem	An opportunity
	Mistake	Learning experience
	Negative	Positive
	Limited	Abundance
Mind choices (Feel)	External control	Internal control
	Timid	Brave
	Weak	Strong
	Indecisive	Certain
	Tense	Calm
	Pessimistic	Optimistic
	Defeated	Encouraged
	Victim	Conqueror
Body choices (Do/Act)	Dream	Plan
	Follow	Lead
	Risk-averse	Calculated risks
	Stagnate	Mature
	Procrastinate	Act
	Blame others	Take responsibility
	Reactive	Proactive
TOTAL	**Life by Default**	**Life by Design**
LIFE GRADE	**Fail**	**Pass**

The table above shows our potential life grade according to the choices we've made in terms of our thoughts, feelings and actions. Take a look at each row in the table and check off whether you fall into the FearFULL or PowerFULL category for each one. How many of your "Think" choices are FearFULL rather than PowerFULL? How many of your "Feel" choices are FearFULL rather than PowerFULL? And lastly, how many of your "Act" choices are FearFULL rather than PowerFULL? Do you have more FearFULL items than PowerFULL items checked off in the entire table? Based on the number of items that you've checked off within each category, you'll be able to determine your self-assessed grade in life thus far. Are you passing or failing to live the life you're capable of living based on how you habitually think, feel, and behave?

FEAR FACT #41: Your life outcomes are the result of the type of energy you've attached to your thoughts, feelings and actions. The law of attraction allows you to attract positive things to yourself if you make the conscious choice to think, feel and act powerFULLy.

In teaching university students, my job also included having to evaluate their performance on exams. I had to determine whether or not they demonstrated knowledge of the material they were taught and assign them a grade. When I was managing corporate teams, my role also included conducting annual performance appraisals of my staff. Did they perform their job requirements or not? They were rated and could receive a monetary bonus based on their job performance. In each case, whether they were my students or my staff, an individual's performance needed to be evaluated based on certain criteria. In each of these roles, I was also evaluated with respect to my ability to perform to expectations. Evaluation was unavoidable.

Did you know that you're also being evaluated in life? I'm not talking about being evaluated by your boss, your teacher, your friends and family, or even the strangers you interact with throughout your day. I'm taking about the way you evaluate yourself. Every day you evaluate yourself on a subconscious level and give yourself a pass-fail grade on the way you're conducting your life; what you're thinking and feeling and how you're acting. The grade you give yourself feeds back into your self-esteem, sense of mastery, and your perception as to whether you're in control of your own life.

When you're in a dysfunctional relationship with Fear, you find that you give yourself a failing grade most, if not all, of the time. That's because you can't pass your life test with Fear standing in your way. Fear never wants you to get a passing life grade; never. He wants to keep you failing because then you'll keep your foggy eye glasses on and remain in a relationship with him. But Power wants you to have a passing life grade and he wants you to pass with flying colors. In fact, he wants you to be the head of the class.

Life is a sum of all the choices you've made up to this point. Some of you might not be so happy with your life grade thus far. But there's good news: it's never too late to take control and live a more determined, self-directed life. It's never too late to start to make better choices that will positively impact your mind, brain, body... and spirit. But in order to do that you need to align all your internal systems for power. You need to make sure that your mind, brain, body and spirit systems are flowing with positive energy, not negative energy. If either one of your internal systems is out of alignment then you won't get the results you're aiming for.

Science meets Spirituality

As a social scientist I'm trained to focus on and make conclusions based on provable and observable scientific facts. In my university training, there was no room for the world of the spiritual; only the cold, hard facts that could be tested and proven within a mathematical statistical model. For a long time that was the world I lived in; that was my reality. However, no matter how much we tried to scientifically calculate the various factors that went into determining a specific outcome, the model was never perfect. It couldn't predict outcomes with absolute certainty. Reality couldn't be reduced to a scientific equation or a collection of theories and testable hypotheses. I felt something was missing in our attempts to gain wisdom from traditional science as we knew it.

Modern society, and its reliance on traditional science for our wisdom, has hindered our ability to see the big picture. It has caused us to be blind to the fact that we're infinitely more powerful than we appear to be. If we rely on science to explain all phenomena and dismiss all experience that can't be calculated or mapped out in a provable theory based on physical laws then we miss the boat. We need to open our mind and broaden our framework about what we believe is real. That's the only way we can grow into our full awareness.

For example, centuries ago, before the invention of the microscope, people didn't know about micro-organisms and their ability to cause disease and death. When someone came down with a disease, common perception was that it was caused by a curse, evil spirits or some other supernatural phenomenon. It was only when the technology was developed to allow us to see and prove the existence of micro-organisms that people saw evidence that it wasn't a curse but bacteria or viruses that caused certain diseases. These tiny but powerful micro-organisms were there all along, it's just that we couldn't see them at the time.

Similarly, dismissing the spiritual realm simply because we haven't as yet been able to provide tangible scientific evidence for all of reality also leads us astray. There are so many things in our world that are simply beyond our current ability to capture them through the lens of modern science. However, some areas of science are just now beginning to develop new approaches to the exploration of human behavior using a new framework that links the world of science with the world of spirituality and consciousness. This approach is finally beginning to realize that we're more than intellectual or emotional beings, we're also spiritual beings. And within our spiritual being lie our greatest strength, our greatest power and our greatest potential.

Although I'm doubtful that spiritual concepts such as universal energy will ever be captured and quantified within a mathematical scientific model, I'm happy to see that some headway is being made in some disciplines to incorporate a holistic approach to learning about human nature. The more that people realize the power that universal energy and the subconscious mind holds, the better our chances of using that energy to improve our lives and the lives of others.

The power of spirit and universal energy has given me more proof of what I'm capable of accomplishing than all the university degrees and specialized training certificates that line the walls of my office. These pieces of paper demonstrate that I've achieved a level of expert knowledge in the fields they represent, but they say nothing about the level of wisdom I've achieved.

My wisdom and personal power came from using my mind to grow in self-awareness and to use what I learned in all areas, academic and spiritual, towards improving not only my life, but the lives of others. That's the purpose of universal energy. Universal energy allows us to operate beyond the material world, beyond the things we can detect with our five senses or by using mathematical scientific models. Our brain and body are physical entities but our mind is non-physical and it's there, in our subconscious mind, where we'll find wisdom. As the famous quote by Ralph Waldo Emerson states: "Before we acquire great power we must acquire the wisdom to use it well."

There's a peace that comes with the knowledge that you're not alone; that you can rely on an infinite power source to help you through life. It took me almost 40 years to find comfort in my dependence on something outside of myself. I was, and still am, a typical Type A personality with all the characteristics that come with it. I'm motivated, independent, goal-oriented, and love mastering new things and overcoming challenges. I have a solid internal locus of control. Although those characteristics are appreciated in our society and in many ways we're conditioned to operate on this level, it can get in the way of our ability to tap into and benefit from universal energy. We're so geared towards doing things by ourselves, relying solely on our own effort, that we don't take advantage of an unlimited power source that's available to help us get what we want more effectively and efficiently.

That's not to say that reliance on universal energy switches your locus of control from internal to external; no indeed. The control is still strictly yours. You make the choice about whether or not you want to benefit from this unlimited power and you make the choice about how much of that power you want to help you supplement your own personal power. Remember, you're a part of a larger system and your internal systems run on universal energy. If you decide to learn how to use this resource, then things will be easier for you. But if you decline to use it, then you'll end up wasting a lot of time and effort relying only on your own personal energy to overcome your fears and get the successful life of your dreams.

For example, let's say that you're on a 10-speed bicycle and attempting to race up a very steep hill. Other people are beside you at the bottom of that very steep hill, also on their 10-speed bicycles. At the top of the hill lies a reward; the reward of a fearless and successful life where you're in control of your own destiny. As the race begins you start to pedal your bicycle. You focus and apply all the strength you have in your legs to move the bicycle forwards and upwards. You're struggling but there's only a slight forward movement. You take a moment to glance to your left and to your right and notice that you're completely alone; that the other riders are already half-way up the hill. What's happening? You all have the same 10-speed bicycles and they're all the same make and model. Why is it so much easier for them to get up the hill? Why are they getting closer to the goal so much faster than you are despite the fact that you're peddling as hard as you can?

Like your internal systems, there's nothing wrong with the quality or the design of your bicycle. The problem lies elsewhere, in the function or the application. Essentially, you're using the bicycle all wrong. In your bicycle is the potential for 10 speeds. Each time you change gears, the bicycle gets easier to maneuver up the steep hill. But unbeknownst to you, you've been struggling in first gear. All your focus and strength hasn't been getting you to the top of the hill — your goal — very quickly or effortlessly at all. You need to do what the others who are already half-way up the hill are doing. They've increased the power of their bicycle by gearing up. They're using less of their own strength and power and are getting up the hill faster and more efficiently than you are. They're relying on the power of the gears which is a greater power source and not just on their own physical power to get them up the hill.

In life, when you fail to gear up you're failing to tap into universal power and you essentially spend your life living in first gear. At that rate it'll take a lifetime, if ever, for you to get up that hill. And while you struggle, others have reached the top, have overcome their fears, and are living the life of their dreams. You have the exact same bicycle as they do; so that's no excuse. You just aren't using your bicycle as effectively as they are and you've paid the price for it in wasted time and effort. *Stop going through your life in first gear.* You have at your disposal the power of the universe to help you increase your own personal power exponentially. Your have inside you a subconscious mind that's a direct link to this universal power source.

> **FEAR FACT #42**: You're a spiritual being as well as an intellectual and emotional being. Using the power of spirit and universal energy is where you'll find your greatest power and reach your greatest potential.

I'm reminded of an old story that was told to me several years ago. In that story, several gods were arguing over where to hide the secret of life so that humans would never discover it. One god said "Let's bury it under a mountain. The humans will never think of looking for it there." But the others opposed that idea saying that eventually the humans would find a way to dig under the mountain and find it. With that idea rejected, another god came up with the idea of hiding the secret of life under the deepest ocean. He said "Let's sink it into the depths of the ocean. No one will ever think of looking for it there." But, like the first suggestion, this one was rejected as well. The other gods said that eventually humans would one day find a way to mine the depths of the oceans and would eventually stumble upon the secret of life. Finally, one god said "Let's put the secret of life *inside the humans*. They'll never, ever think of looking for it there." All the gods loved this idea and agreed that this would be the most ideal hiding place for the secret of life.

The secret of life then is that *your ultimate power is already within you.* You don't have to go looking for it anywhere. Like the famous quote by Joseph Campbell states "The cave you fear to enter holds the treasure you seek." Many people are afraid of inner searching; they're afraid of what they might find and so spend their lives living superficially with little or no introspection or self-awareness. They'd rather focus on temporary "fixes" like getting stylish clothes, new hairstyles, expensive cars, and other external attempts to feel good about themselves. But these attempts at making themselves feel better don't last very long at all. In fact, they invariably fail to fix anything because they don't get to the root of dysfunctional thoughts, feelings and behaviors in their internal systems.

Your spirit and connection with your universal power source is the permanent fix for your thoughts, feelings and actions. A holistic approach is the only way to achieve your full potential and live a powerFULL and fearLESS life of your own design. It's the only way you'll get an unshakable internal locus of control, heightened self-awareness and unlimited positive energy. If you fail to grasp this concept then everything discussed in *Dump Your Fear!* will be of significantly less value to you.

I want you make to the conscious choice to use the gifts that lie within you to overcome your fears and claim your personal power. It's the only way that you'll be able to fulfill the universal command that every living thing exists to reach its full potential; not merely for its own sake, but for the sake of us all. Don't let your fears prevent you from reaching your full potential. Don't spend the rest of your life struggling in first gear.

Chapter Eleven
Power Tools

"No amount of reading or memorizing will make you successful in life.
It is the understanding and application of wise thought which counts."
Bob Proctor

"To know and not to do is not to know."
Chinese Proverb

"You'll never plough a field by turning it over in your mind."
Irish Proverb

Congratulations! You've gotten through the previous ten chapters and have learned and have become aware of why you have the fears you do and how they've been impacting your thoughts, feelings, actions, and life outcomes. You've also discovered secrets about the unlimited power of your subconscious mind to change the way your internal systems operate by tapping into unlimited universal energy. It's likely something you never really took the time to consider in any great detail before. But, it's essential that you became aware of *why* you have the fears you do, and *how* they impact your life before you could make a conscious decision to decide *what* you need to do to overcome them.

Over the course of the previous ten chapters, you've been presented with material that will allow you to get rid of the old negative conditioning that has wired your brain and your mind for fear. You've learned important concepts in mental health, neuroscience, biology and even spirituality and have been show principles that will equip you to do just that. You've discovered that a mind-brain-body-spirit approach that addresses your fears from a systems perspective will transform your thoughts, feelings, actions and thus the results you want. Perhaps, like many of my clients, you've tried other methods before and haven't been successful at overcoming your fears and achieving the level of success you want in your relationships, or your personal or professional life. But now you know that since every human being consists of interdependent and interconnected systems and that trying to change one part of yourself without addressing and changing the others is bound to fail (e.g., like trying to change your behaviors without addressing your underlying thoughts and feelings).

By now you've significantly increased your knowledge and perhaps have grown in your self-awareness of how the material discussed applies to your specific fears and your specific life circumstances. Now what? What happens next? Well, *what must happen next is action: you must apply the principles.* Reading about them and even thinking about them without taking action does nothing to move you further toward achieving the successful life you long for. Just like the electric power tools that you may have in your home, like a power drill, tools can only perform their intended function to the extent that you use them. A drill laying in the garage collecting dust, or in a closet in the box it came with, does nothing to get the nails into the wall so that you can hang up your pictures. As long as the drill stays unused, the pictures will remain unhung and your home will not be as beautiful as it could be. It won't have reached its full potential.

The same goes for the tools and principles that I've used throughout this book. You need to use what you've learned to *Dump Your Fear!* and embrace your personal power. You need to take action. You need to use your Power Tools and Power-Up (see Chapter Twelve for "Power-Up" How-To's). You need to get to the Action stage of the "Stages of Change" chart (in Chapter Eight) so you can fully incorporate the principles into your internal system and progress to the next level.

One of the effects of being in a dysfunctional relationship with Fear is that people tend to procrastinate — to avoid making choices; to put things off rather than taking immediate action. Did you know that *procrastination is really a fear of failing*? That's right. Procrastinators fear that their attempts will fail and so they avoid taking action so they don't prove themselves right. But by now you know that this is a self-fulfilling prophesy of thoughts leading to feelings, feelings leading to actions (remember, failure to act is still an action), and actions leading to results.

You now know that in order to prove to yourself that you won't fail, that you actually have to act; to do the thing you fear. As the famous quote by Ralph Waldo Emerson states: "Do the thing you fear and the death of fear is certain". Taking action is the only way that the foggy eye glasses that Fear has put on you will fall off for good. Taking action is the only way that you'll see that your self-imposed limits, your learned helplessness, your habitual fearful responses are just a function of your conditioning and the information you've stored about yourself in your subconscious mind and are all under your conscious control.

So you need to make a decision NOW to take action; to move your thoughts and feelings about finally overcoming your fears into action. By reading this book, you've already begun to rid yourself of the fear virus that has infected your internal systems. The words you've read have been added to your brain's "memory bank" and the energy stored as permanent memories in your subconscious mind. Now it's up to you to use your conscious mind to propel you towards overcoming your fears and towards the successful life that you dream of.

Using Your "Power Tools"

In my professional practice as a life transformational coach and mindset mentor I deal with people's fears quite frequently. Many of the roadblocks in their way of success stem from their inability to overcome some fear barrier or another. In helping my clients overcome their fear barriers, I'm able to conduct individual assessments to determine how specifically their thoughts, feelings and behaviors have been uniquely shaped by their own and others' fear-conditioning and how deeply their fears have been wired into their brain and subconscious mind. I can also assess the extent to which their fears are getting in the way of their personal relationships, their ability to succeed at work, their health, friendships and other aspects of their lives.

I use a variety of tools to help my clients overcome their fears and embrace their personal power. The "Power Tools" I choose depend largely on my assessment of the client (e.g., the type of fears they struggle with; their readiness to implement the principles; their level of self-awareness, etc.). No single method is always successful in overcoming fear and what works for one person may not work for another. Because of this, I use a combination of approaches with my clients and start off with basic exercises and gradually build up the level of difficulty so that they can achieve mastery at each level before moving on to the next.

Clients need to demonstrate mastery at earlier levels in both their knowledge and in the application of the tools, before I allow them to move on to higher, more complex levels. In attempting to overcome your fears, it may take you a bit of time and practice to develop competency at each level depending on the type of fear you're experiencing and the extent to which it has impacted your mind, brain, body systems. But be patient. It took time for Fear to infect your internal systems and it'll take a bit of time to get him out. But the time it'll take to get him out is only a tiny fraction of the length of time you've been in a dysfunctional relationship with him.

Know that, like everyone who has undertaken the journey from fearFULL to powerFULL (including me), as you attempt to overcome your fears you'll undoubtedly encounter fear barriers and want to think, feel and act in your old habitual ways. For the most part you developed fear-based thinking, feeling and behaving out of habit; out of repeatedly giving in to fear. That is, you acted out of fear once, then twice, then multiple times. Each time you did this, you inadvertently reinforced your fear response in your brain and your subconscious mind. So it's now a part of your subconscious emotional predispositions as well as your conscious thoughts and behavioral response to stressors.

Since it took hundreds, if not hundreds of thousands of repeated fear-based thoughts, feelings and actions to develop your fear habit, it'll take more than one attempt to overcome this conditioning that has worked like a virus in your internal systems. You'll need to use the *power of repetition* to form new habits which will rewire new neural pathways in your brain and reprogram your subconscious mind with new paradigms. Don't give up at the first setback or the first time you find yourself falling back into old wired fearful patterns. You'll have to go through these momentary feelings of discomfort to achieve the re-conditioning and breakthroughs that will move you from a state of fear into a state of empowerment.

You may initially feel like trying to overcome your fear habit is like adding another stressor to your life. That's because overcoming established habits causes the brain, mind and body to feel stressed (you might, for example, know a smoker who went through withdrawal symptoms and became cranky and short-tempered while they were trying to quit). As you now know, exposure to stressors causes an automatic fight-or-flight response in your brain.

When you first attempt to change your thoughts, feelings and behaviors, your internal systems may actually perceive your new attempts as a form of stress. That's because you're doing something new and unfamiliar. Things that are new and take us out of our comfort zone (even when we consciously seek out these experiences) can sometimes cause us to feel fearful or anxious. But don't give in to any temptation to *flee* from your decision to change and transform your life from fearFULL to powerFULL. Remember, you have the power of your mind and the logical part of your brain (your prefrontal cortex) to do what's necessary to avoid the amygdala hijack and to persevere in your attempts to *Dump Your Fear!* Moreover, you have the unlimited power of the universe to help your subconscious mind keep you on the path to success.

You may find yourself over the course of a single day, needing to pull yourself back several times from your fearFULL thoughts. That's okay. You need to be prepared to do battle with yourself at first as you reprogram your internal systems and switch your energy from negative to positive. It will get easier; trust me. You're actually in the process of practicing to be the new powerFULL you, and practicing is what leads to a solid and lasting transformation. Like the famous quote from Larry Gelwix the famous winning rugby coach says: "practice makes permanent".

Each time you mentally give yourself a shake and re-direct your thinking, you'll be establishing new neural pathways and positive new emotions in your subconscious mind. This will rewire your brain and give new instructions to your subconscious mind and you'll gradually begin to consistently think, feel, and act with less fear. This will be your new way of thinking, feeling and behaving for the rest of your life. As a result, you'll find that your life outcomes will improve significantly as the law of attraction kicks into action to bring positive things your way.

Know that after reading *Dump Your Fear!* you are well able to:

- Take yourself through an assessment of your knowledge and awareness of your fears;
- Incorporate how they influence your thoughts, feelings and actions into your level of self-awareness;
- Determine your readiness to change from fearFULL to powerFULL;
- Align your subconscious and conscious mind with your intention to overcome your dysfunctional relationship with Fear
- Get your internal systems working in harmony with universal energy; and,
- Apply the principles and tools that you've learned to all aspects of your personal and professional life so that you can get on the path to overcoming your fears and live the successful life you've always dreamed of.

I've filled *Dump Your Fear!* with many essential "must have" bits of knowledge, wisdom, and takeaways that I acquired from a lifetime of personal experience; formal education at the Master's and doctoral levels including concepts related to mental health, biology and neuroscience; specialized training in a variety of fields related to the power of the mind and spiritual growth; and, over 25 years of coaching individuals and corporate teams to overcome barriers to their success.

By reading this book, you'll benefit from my years of pain and struggle to find the answers to the problem of overcoming fear, hundreds of thousands of dollars spent on formal university education and specialized training, and all the lessons-learned from my own and others' personal experiences. You have in *Dump Your Fear!* a lifetime of knowledge and wisdom to use as your personal transformational coach to help put you on the path to overcoming your fears.

Although I'm not able to provide an exhaustive list of all the "Power Tools" I use with my clients or a comprehensive step-by-step guide about how you'd implement each of them here (*Dump Your Fear!* would go on for hundreds of pages more), I do provide you with the essentials — the common denominators — that everyone needs to have in their Power Tool box, regardless of the type of fears they face.

I've developed a "Top Ten" list of Power Tools as a brief summary for you with the essential "common denominators". Use these in conjunction with the information contained in the "Power-Up How-To's" in the next chapter to take you from fearFULL to powerFULL. Commit to making the change. Commit to starting down the road to overcoming your fears and reaching your full potential. Commit to you! **Commit to *Dump Your Fear!***

Top 10 Ways to Achieve Your Positive Power

1. *Get to know yourself as a distinct and unique individual* and grow in self-awareness.
    *   You are a unique gift of the universe and put on earth to contribute your unique talents towards your self-actualization and towards helping others.

- Don't let your fears define who you think you are. You are not your fears.

- Discover your own unique values, attitudes and beliefs and learn how they influence your thoughts, feelings and actions.

2. ***Develop your will.*** Your conscious will is what will push you to do things, to generate the actions necessary to overcome your fears.

  - When you have a strong will you'll be goal-oriented and determined to get whatever you set your mind to. You'll be the actor in your life (i.e., life by design) rather than be acted upon (i.e., life by default). You'll be an instrumentalist, with an internal locus of control and high self-efficacy.

  - A strong will is what will allow you to effectively manage you internal systems and align them to carry out your new PowerFULL self-programming.

3. ***Take personal responsibility for your actions*** and their outcomes. Although we can't always control how people treat us or the situations we find ourselves in, we are always in control of the way we respond to them. Be sure to visit **www.wired2succeed.com** for more information on how to stop making excuses and take personal responsibility for your actions.

  - Rather than blaming situations or people for your thoughts, feelings or actions, you need to realize that inputs from your external systems don't automatically mean that you must respond in a certain way with your internal systems.

- You have a choice about whether or not you think, feel and act with fear.

- You grow in power and self-esteem when you accept complete responsibility for the decisions you've made and the current circumstances in your life.

4. ***Exercise your power of choice***. When you were living in a dysfunctional relationship with Fear, he made all the choices for you. Now the choices are yours. Be sure to visit **www.wired2succeed.com** for more information on how to exercise your power of choice.

   - Choose to say "no" to the things and people in your life that don't line up with your new sense of self and new FearLESS paradigms.

   - Choose to pay attention to your own needs and desires, not just the needs of others. In fact, without being selfish, you need to make your needs a priority because until your own needs are met, you can't truly and freely give yourself to others. Remember, whenever you fly, the flight attendants instruct passengers to put on their own mask first before attending to the needs of others. That's because if you fail to attend to your needs first and something happens that causes you to lose control of your internal systems, you can't help anyone else at all. It's not a selfish act but a practical act; attending to others without attending to yourself as well puts you and them at risk. That is also a valuable lesson for how you should live your life.

   - Choose to focus on the positive things in life rather than the negative. Remember, the law of attraction is always at work.

5. *Create a "power journal"* where each day you write down one specific way that you intend to be FearLESS and PowerFULL that day.

   - Each day, choose a specific word or write a brief description about how you want to feel. This is your intention; your goal for the day for achieving positive power. Align your actions with your thoughts and feelings.
   - Each week, use the power journal to track your progress. By reflecting on your progress, you'll see that you've consistently thought, felt and acted more powerfully as time goes on.
   - Use this evidence to boost your level of self-awareness, your will and your internal locus of control and set new, higher goals for yourself.

6. *Harness the power of positive affirmations.* Positive affirmations have the power to change your self-talk which can change the way you think and feel about yourself. Remember, thoughts and words are energy.

   - Affirmations are all about allowing positive energy to flow though your internal systems and out into the universe.
   - Make a commitment to say your positive affirmations out loud at least twice a day. Remember, repetition will allow your brain and your subconscious mind to reprogram themselves.
   - Say things like "I am a fearless person who's in control and fully able to get from life what I want." When you

speak words of positivity to yourself and to the universe, the law of attraction is set in motion.

7. ***Practice positive self-talk** and **positive thinking***. Make sure that what you say to yourself (your self-talk) is always self-respecting, affirming and positive. Be sure to visit **www.wired2succeed.com** for more information on how to stay positive.

- Words (even those spoken just "in your head") are full of energy and will set the law of attraction in motion.

- Positive self-talk will also give you confidence by impressing your new FearLESS image of yourself into your subconscious mind.

- Whenever you experience an automatic negative reaction to someone or something, take a few seconds to breathe deeply and clear your mind and think of at least one thing that is positive about the situation or person.

8. ***Visualize yourself living the FearLESS successful life of your dreams and take progressive steps towards that goal***. Remember the brain and subconscious mind makes no distinction between what is real and what is imagined. Please be sure to visit **www.wired2succeed.com** for more information on how to use visualization.

- As you visualize and imagine what you want out of life, you are in essence, harnessing the power of your brain and your subconscious mind to get to work creating your vision in real life.

- Your subconscious mind is what links you to unlimited universal energy, which is unlimited power. So when you direct your mind to do something, it pulls the unlimited power from the universe that you can use as your own personal power source to create the very thing you've visualized.

- Vision without action is inaction. Thoughts and feelings without action can't lead to results. So make sure to set goals that line up with the image you have of yourself and chip away at them each day.

9. *Be careful about the quality of your external systems.* When you first make the decision to move from fearFULL to powerFULL, you may be surprised that not everyone you know is happy about your planned changes. Your family, friends, work colleagues, team members, neighbors, etc. have become accustomed the old you and may feel threatened by your new sense of purpose and increased self-esteem. Overcoming your own fears is a fear-trigger for them (for example, they may begin to see themselves in a new light as their relationship with you goes through a period of adjustment).

- Do not let this be another source of stress and fear for you. Keep your mind focused on reprogramming your internal systems for power.
- Try to get buy-in by letting them know that as you become a more fearLESS and empowered they'll also benefit. Let them know that you're willing to include them in your journey and as you grow in personal power and control, you'll be better positioned to help them succeed in their own lives.
- Read inspirational books and attend inspirational seminars or webinars (like the kind you'll find on

www.wired2succeed.com). There you'll find like-minded individuals and materials that will support your decision to move from fearFULL to powerFULL.

10. *Always look for ways to help others.* Direct your positive energy outwards, not just inwards. One of the blessings of achieving personal power is that we're able to share what we've learned, and what we've become, with others who are still struggling.

- Be a blessing to others in your family, your community or elsewhere in the world. Universal energy and power have no limits and, because we benefit from them, our power and energy are unlimited as well.

- We don't lose power when we consciously choose to help others; instead, we grow in our power and energy as the universe rewards us with abundance.

- Every day take the opportunity to do something nice for someone else. Whether it's opening a door for someone on your way into a building, making it easier for someone to merge into heavy traffic, or even saying "please" and "thank you" to the person who serves you coffee, you'll be helping to make others' feel better about themselves and their day. Most people are happy to "play it forward" and be nice to others in response to having someone — like you — be nice to them.

Chapter Twelve
It's Time to Power-Up: The "How-To's"

"To change who you are, change who you think you are."
Jonathan Lockwood Huie

"Understand that the right to choose your own path is a sacred privilege. Use it. Dwell in possibility."
Oprah Winfrey

"As long as you live, you'll keep 'becoming'. Never make the mistake of thinking that you've reached your full potential. That's the beauty of living."
Jacinth Tracey

Throughout this book I've used terms, concepts and proven scientific principles, particularly in the fields of biology and neuroscience (e.g., fight-or-flight response, neural pathways, neuroplasticity, etc.), mental health and psychology (e.g., conditioning, locus of control, self-esteem, etc.), and spirituality (e.g., self-awareness, mindfulness, universal energy, etc.). A working familiarity with these concepts is essential for you to understand how fear has evolved as a patterned response in your thoughts, feelings and actions and what steps you must take to eliminate the "fear virus" from your internal systems.

You needed to come to terms with your own fears, to confront them at their source, and understand just how destructive your dysfunctional relationship with Fear has been for your mind, brain, body and spirit before you could consciously embark on the path to healing your internal systems and overcoming your fears.

In this chapter I've provided you with more details about these concepts, and specific instructions about how to apply them to help you overcome your dysfunctional relationship with Fear. It's essential that you develop more healthy and functional thoughts, feelings and actions in order to *Dump Your Fear!*. Remember, your thoughts lead to feelings; your feelings lead to actions; and your actions ultimately determine what you get out of life.

Throughout this book, you've discovered the importance of using a holistic approach. It's the only way you'll be able to reprogram the old conditioning that has made you vulnerable to Fear. It's the only way you'll get the fear virus out of your internal systems. You've learned that since Fear influences your mind, brain, and body that you need to pay attention to each of these parts of you. Ignoring one part will not get you your desired results. For example, focusing on reprogramming your brain (i.e., though behavior modification) without paying attention to how your subconscious mind influences your brain, will only get you minimal results.

As well, focusing only on alleviating the physiological symptoms of fear (like the elevated heart rate, rapid breathing, etc. that happens during fight-or-flight arousal) will also only get you minimal results. That's because medications are not a cure for your fear response; they only treat the symptoms, not the underlying cause. They don't address your core belief systems and habitual patterned responses that are, in actuality, the root causes of your fears. Medications don't help you become self-aware and don't help you connect with your universal source of power. As such, focusing on how your body responds when you experience fear is only part of the puzzle.

Over the course of almost 30 years, I've worked in both adolescent psychiatry and geriatric psychiatry and have seen the positive and negative effects of medication to alleviate psychiatric symptoms. I've seen in-patients who were initially a danger to themselves and/or others when admitted to the hospital do very well when given the proper dosage to manage their symptoms. I've also seen patients who become dependent on their medication and the uncomfortable side effects they experience as their dosage increases over time in order to keep their symptoms at bay. I've also seen what happens when patients who are medication-dependent fail to take their medication, and because they have no other coping strategies, their illness overtakes them. In addition, most if not all medications (natural or otherwise) have side-effects, even if they are well-tolerated. Eventually, many types of medication will accumulate in the liver and kidneys.

So, I have a healthy respect for both the pros and cons of using medication as a tool to cope with mental health issues. In cases of significant distress or psychiatric disorder, medication is generally the only initial way to alleviate symptoms. But what I am advocating here is that prescription drugs or self-medicating (e.g., by using alcohol or other substances) not be used as a singular long-term coping strategy, especially when it comes to the types of fear we've been discussing. Remember, our thoughts, feelings and behaviors are a complex interplay between our physical and social selves (i.e., our internal systems interact with our external systems to create our reality).

Drug therapies, therefore, in my opinion, should generally be used to provide short-term help (such as helping with severe panic attacks) and not as a long-term solution to dealing with fears. During my initial meetings with clients, I always ask if they're currently using, or have recently used, medication to alleviate their fear symptoms. Depending on the severity of their fear, or the length of time they've been dependent on the medication, I work with them to combine their existing treatment with a more holistic approach.

A holistic mind-brain-body-spirit approach recognizes the importance of systems to the creation and maintenance of your fears. Because your systems are interdependent and interact with each other, focusing on just your body system alone generally disrupts other parts of your system like your brain and your mind. For example, if you come to believe that the only way to deal with your fear is to take medication, then your locus of control is external; it's the medication not you that's doing the work. The power is in the pill, not in you. As you now know, people with an external locus of control tend to have lower self-esteem, mastery and tend to be more fatalistic in their approach to life. This in turn impacts their behaviors which influences their outcomes.

I really want you to develop a relationship with your own personal power. To do that, you need to Power-Up. In the video game world, "power-up" means that extra abilities, or powers, are given to a character. It transforms the character by giving it more powerful tools to take on threats and challenges. It makes the character less vulnerable to attack. The character can power-up by defeating an enemy or by performing certain actions. You'll be able to power-up by dumping Fear (i.e., defeating an enemy) and by performing the actions of increasing your self-awareness, your self-esteem, developing an internal locus of control, and connecting to your universal power source. This is the power-up you'll need to win your game of life.

You are the main character in your own game, in your own life. Only you can decide if you want to keep playing the game like you've always done and getting the same poor results you always have. The only way to get better at the game, to go on to eliminate your fears and get the successful life of your dreams, is to change the way you've been playing the game. It's time to Power-Up with these "How-To's".

I've listed five of the numerous "How-To's" that are available at **www.wired2succeed.com**. Again, *Dump Your Fear!* would go on for numerous more pages were I to try to list all the relevant "How-To's" here. For more information about such things as: how to use visualization and guided imagery; how to stay positive; how to stop making excuses and take personal responsibility for your life; how to set and achieve your goals, etc. please be sure to visit **www.wired2succeed.com**. There you'll find additional information about overcoming fear barriers; **a gift of $500 worth of FREE online video and audio training; updates about my upcoming seminars and webinars, and much more**.

How to Increase Your Self-Awareness

Self-awareness is defined as the ability to be introspective; to see yourself as a unique object in the world and apart from other people in terms of your traits, feelings and behaviors. You grow in self-awareness over the course of your entire life. You never stop becoming the person you were created to be. That's because life is continually providing you with lessons to tweak and improve yourself, and giving you opportunities to incorporate these new lessons into the person you've already become.

In order to overcome your fears, and indeed to keep growing as a person, you need to keep learning, to keep "becoming", no matter how old you are or how much you've learned about yourself and your role in the world. This is a good thing. Imagine how boring and unmotivated we would all be if we could one day sit back and say: "I guess that's it. I know everything there is to know about myself." Getting to know yourself at deeper and deeper levels is one of the most wonderful gifts that life has given you. Because the universe is unlimited in energy and power, you'll keep growing in energy, power and self-awareness as long as you keep tapping into this energy source. Remember, it's by using your subconscious mind that you can tap into universal power, and it's by using your conscious and subconscious mind that you'll grow in self-awareness and overcome your fears.

Self-awareness is key to having the gears in your internal systems move efficiently and effectively. It's what will allow you to monitor and adjust your thoughts, feelings and actions so that you can overcome your fears, improve your relationships, and reach your personal and professional goals with less time and energy. You increase your self-awareness when you:

1. ***Take the time to relax or meditate*** to get in touch with your thoughts and feelings. Silence is a powerful tool in the development of self-awareness. It is in the silent moments that, without outside distraction, you're able to direct your attention inwards (see "How to Achieve Mindfulness" section in this chapter). That's because you slow your brain waves and reduce the interference from your conscious mind. You're then free to attend to the interaction and energy exchange between your subconscious mind and your universal power source.

2. ***Ask yourself questions.*** The questions and information in this book have been designed to help you along the path to increasing your self-awareness. For example, you now understand that your past conditioning and your current dysfunctional relationship with Fear has influenced your life outcomes based on the way you've thought, felt and acted thus far. You're now aware that you can make the conscious choices to reprogram yourself and eliminate the fear virus from your systems at any time. You're now

aware that you need to act, not just think about overcoming your fear to get the successful life you want. You're now aware that you have an unlimited source of power to help you overcome your fears and so you don't have to do it alone. You're now aware that your subconscious mind holds the key to determining what triggers your fears. When you start to think fearful thoughts or about to react with fear, stop and ask yourself the following questions:

    a) What am I thinking?

    b) What am I feeling?

    c) What do I feel like doing as a result of the way I'm thinking and feeling?

    d) Is my response reasonable?

    e) What can I do other than give in to my fearful thoughts and feelings?

3. *Ask others questions about you.* Sometimes we don't know what we don't know, especially when we're just starting down the path towards self-awareness. So, it might be helpful for you to get feedback about yourself from someone you trust. For example, if you think that you're a calm, reasoned person but when you ask your close friends and family they all say that you're a quick-tempered hot-head, then that tells you something. Ask them to give you specific examples of why they believe certain things about you. Examine how their view of you lines up with your view of yourself.

4. *Keep an "awareness journal".* By keeping a journal of your thoughts and feelings, you might be able to see patterns that you'd otherwise miss. Making notes will not only give you an opportunity to identify and label your feelings, and a chance to see how those feelings have

influenced your behaviors and your outcomes, but you'll be able to better modify your thoughts, feelings and behaviors as necessary. For example, you now know that sometimes your subconscious mind may react to a fear trigger well before the trigger is perceived by your conscious mind or your brain. By documenting your thoughts, feelings and actions and what has preceded them, you'll be better able to identify your fear triggers (see "How to take a Fear trigger Audit" section in this chapter).

5. *Try new things and put yourself in new situations.* When we keep doing the same things or encounter the same situations over and over again, our thoughts, feelings and behaviors often become automatic (just like when we drive a car after years of driving, we don't always consciously pay attention to the mechanics of driving because our conditioned responses have become automatic). As you now know, your fears can become automatic as well. It's when we put ourselves into new situations, learn new things, or face new challenges that we often discover new things about ourselves. The novelty of new situations and new knowledge prompts us to try to understand ourselves better. For example, you might ask yourself "Why does this new situation make me feel fearful?" or "How does my fearful feeling about this situation or this person relate to my fear about a certain other situation or a certain other person in my life?"

How to Increase Your Internal Locus of Control

Locus of control is where someone places their attributions; whether they believe that their efforts make a difference (internal locus of control) or whether they believe that their efforts make little difference to their life outcomes because most things are outside of their control (external locus of control).

As you now know, having an internal locus of control is extremely important to overcoming your fears. You must first recognize the fact that you have a choice about how you want to live your life. Do you want to have other people make the choices for you (life by default), or do you want to be the one making the choices for how your life unfolds (life by design)? These are the only two options because making no choice is essentially making the choice to let others make choices for you.

When you have an internal locus of control you think, feel and act like you have the power to take control of your fears and determine what direction you want your life to take. Because thoughts lead to feelings, feelings lead to actions, and actions lead to results, people with an internal locus of control tend to work harder and persevere longer to get what they want. People who are successful in their relationships and in their personal and professional lives have an internal locus of control. You will need to have an internal locus of control in order to move from fearFULL to powerFULL.

By consciously adopting an internal locus of control (by using the powers of your conscious mind to tell your subconscious mind and your brain how you think and feel about yourself and your ability to control your life) you set the gears of re-conditioning in motion, you help to rid your system of the fear virus. You can develop an internal locus of control when you:

1. *Set goals for yourself.* When you set goals and work towards achieving them, this provides your subconscious mind with new positive information that helps you to develop new paradigms; new ways of thinking, feeling and behaving. With each goal accomplished, you boost

your sense of mastery, self-esteem and sense of control over your life outcomes. Research shows that people with an internal locus of control tend to plan for long-term goals and are more likely to work hard to achieve success compared to those with an external locus of control. Please be sure to visit **www.wired2succeed.com** for more information about how to set and achieve your goals.

2. *Eliminate the negative self-talk.* What you say to yourself is what you think about yourself, and it has an impact on the way you feel and behave. What you say to yourself has energy. If you say nice things to yourself, you're not only programming the paradigms in your subconscious mind, you're also sending out positive energy into the universe which in turns sends that energy back to you in the form of positive results in your life. If you say negative things to yourself, the opposite happens and you end up with negative life results. So when you hear yourself saying things like "I always react with fear, I have no choice" or "There's nothing I can do about the fearful way I feel or about my situation" then you need to remind yourself that there's always an element of choice. You may not have any choice about the situation or how other people behave but you always have a choice about whether you choose to think, feel and behave fearfully or powerfully.

3. *Develop skills sets and knowledge that will help boost your self-esteem and mastery.* If you don't know something then find out about it. People with an internal locus of control are more likely to actively seek out information concerning their situation so that they can make informed decisions about how to act. When you seek out and learn new information, this becomes part of

your thought and decision-making process and helps you to make conscious rather than fear-based, emotional decisions. When you make better decisions and act on them, you'll end up with better life outcomes, and this in turn, will reinforce and strengthen your internal locus of control. Overcoming your fears by learning about how you acquired them, their impact on your internal and external systems and what you need to do to overcome them is a great way to develop the skills you need to achieve mastery and increase your self-esteem.

How to Increase Your Self-Esteem

Self-esteem is defined as is the way you think (judgment) and feel (attitude) about yourself in relation to others; it's your emotional evaluation of your own worth. People with low self-esteem tend to see themselves in a generally negative light. Because they have little self-awareness (they don't really know themselves), they let Fear tell them who they are, what to think and feel, and how to act. You can increase your self-esteem when you:

1. ***Take off your foggy eye glasses***. People with low self-esteem tend to be fatalists and have an external locus of control. That is, when something good happens to them they attribute it to luck or outside forces. They don't have a realistic view of themselves as capable of having power and control. When you're in a dysfunctional relationship with Fear, for example, he puts foggy eye glasses on you so you don't see yourself clearly. By taking off your foggy eye glasses you'll be able to grow in self-awareness.

2. ***Stop the negative thinking***. Low self-esteem feeds off the negative thoughts and feelings that you have about

yourself that Fear has made you come to believe. These negative thoughts are negative energy that, through the law of attraction, bring even more negative things to your life. In order to boost your self-esteem you need to see your life outcomes as within your personal control. You need to see "failures" as temporary setbacks and not evidence that you "can't" do something. Don't magnify the setbacks and don't generalize them to reflect who you think you are at your core. For example, if you react with fear to a certain situation, don't think to yourself "Here I go again letting Fear take over my entire life. I react with fear to everything". Instead say "I've had a fear-reaction to a specific thing or a specific situation but that doesn't mean that I react with fear to everything, all the time. I'm on my way to becoming a more fearless person." By constantly reminding yourself of who you want to be rather than who you think you are, you'll focus your energy on the positives rather than the negatives.

3. ***Don't strive to be perfect.*** Striving for success is healthy; we all need to have goals in order to progress and grow. However, striving for perfection in everything we do at all times is a sure way to become frustrated and unmotivated. Because people with low self-esteem tend to take an all-or-none approach (it's either 100% perfect or it's a 100% failure) they tend to miss out on their accomplishments that come close to perfect. Worse still, they don't even reward themselves for having tried. So, instead of giving yourself a 100% failure for the reacting with fear to a particular situation, ask yourself "On a scale of 1-10, with 1 being completely fearful and 10 being completely fearless, how would I rate my reaction to this particular situation?" This forces you to focus on just this

particular situation, rather than making sweeping statements about your fear responses in general. As well, you'll be able to rate yourself on your fear response each time and see that you do indeed vary in scores over time; it's never "all-or-none". That way, you can be free to appreciate yourself for your efforts at overcoming your fears, not just for your results.

4. ***Don't strive to be exactly like someone else;*** strive to be the best you that you can be. As I discussed in Chapter Two, the conditioning that we get from the media and the social comparisons that follow can play havoc with our self-esteem. We see the movie stars, supermodels and the rich-and-famous in all their "perfection" and can begin to criticize ourselves for not being as successful, beautiful, or fit as they are. And in an attempt to be more "perfect" some of us might even try hard to be like them; using them as a standard for what we'd like to become. However, in doing so, we can lose sight of our own unique talents, abilities and qualities. We're all born with our own uniqueness and that's what self-awareness is all about. It provides us with the ability to boost our self-esteem based on our own characteristics, not based on how we compare ourselves to others. So, if for example, you know someone who overcame their fears after having made just one attempt, don't think that you're a failure because you're still in the midst of overcoming yours. Everyone is different in terms of their conditioning, paradigms, motivation, goals, etc. and these play a part in how easy or difficult it is to face and overcome fears. In order to improve your self esteem you need to be the best you that you can be and see yourself as separate and apart from the uniqueness of others. As the famous quote from

Oscar Wilde goes: "Be yourself; everyone else is already taken."

How to Achieve Mindfulness

Mindfulness is defined in many ways but generally refers to an individual's ability to bring their attention to the present moment, on purpose (i.e., consciously) and without making judgments. It's a conscious focus of awareness towards the self. Remember, mindfulness is a part of self-awareness but it's not self-awareness. For example, someone might be aware that they're having a fear response but that doesn't mean that they are mindful of their fear response. In order to be mindful, they need to be purposefully aware of their fear, not just automatically reacting with fear based on their conditioning and paradigms. Realizing that they're experiencing fear is not the same as being mindfully aware that they're experiencing fear. Remember the eating example I spoke about in Chapter Six; you can eat either mindlessly or mindfully. As such, you can either experience fear mindlessly or mindfully.

Children provide us with excellent examples of how to focus and be present in what we do; they're mindful, as we all were as children. When they play, they can focus on one thing while being completely oblivious to outside distractions. However, as we mature and take on responsibilities and a variety of social roles (e.g., parent, employee or boss, husband or wife, etc.), we lose our innate ability to be mindful because we're pulled in so many directions at once. Rather than one object of awareness, we have several. For example, in our busy modern day-to-day life, it's relatively easy to be continually distracted as we multitask and perform one task with our eye towards what we've already done, or what we still need to do later. Our "To Do" list often reflects a seemingly endless number of tasks; each needing to be completed and checked off before we can move on to the other. It's very easy to lose focus on the present moment. We become human "doings" rather than human "beings".

When we lose focus, our brain and subconscious mind can't process information as easily because they're occupied with attending to more than one thing at a time. However, both thrive on focused attention. In particular, our subconscious mind is geared towards attending to one goal and working towards directing universal energy toward the fulfillment of that goal. So, when you shift from one goal to another or multitask from moment to moment, it's more difficult for your subconscious mind to help you achieve any one goal. As such, you need to make a conscious effort to focus, to be present and mindful.

One of the best ways I found to tune out the distractions of my brain and conscious mind is through the practice of yoga. Yoga keeps you in the present moment and keeps you breathing deeply, oxygenating your blood and bringing your attention to the very act of the moment. When your mind wanders you purposefully bring your attention back to your mat. As my yoga instructor is fond of saying at the start of each class: "Nothing exists for the next hour except you and your mat. There is no before and no after, just the present."

When I first began my yoga practice several years ago, I was a busy executive with my days and evenings filled with multitasking and rapidly shifting departmental and corporate priorities. I had a lifelong history of hectic, mindless activity in my personal and professional life; particularly when I was in graduate school and juggling multiple roles. There was always something to do next; something to check off on my "To Do" list that made it difficult to focus on the present moment even when those moments were pleasurable.

So, during the first few months of my yoga practice I didn't get all the benefits of the practice. Yoga isn't just about strengthening the body; it's also about strengthening the mind. This is the spiritual and perhaps most beneficial aspect of the practice. But I found it difficult to be in the moment, for the moment, of the moment when there was always something pressing to do later on. I couldn't quiet my brain and mind long enough to be mindful of my practice; my attention kept wandering away to my "To Do" list even in the midst of holding some very physically challenging yoga postures. In fact, as often is the case, the most difficult yoga pose wasn't headstand or plow or crow, but was shavasana (pronounced she-vas-nah) where after a strenuous practice one lies perfectly still on ones' back on the mat for several minutes and focuses the mind inward to release any remaining tension and reset the body. It requires complete internal awareness and the avoidance of external sensory distractions.

Within the first few months of yoga practice I'd learned to master my body; to manipulate it into positions that I hadn't thought possible. But learning to master shavasana meant learning to master my internal systems. I had to learn to keep my brain from resurrecting my "To Do" list in the midst of my practice, keep my body perfectly still without the restless movement of my arms or legs, and keep my mind from wanting to judge my performance.

It was only in learning to become mindful on my mat that I learned to become mindful in my life. The deep rhythmic yoga breathing provides easier access to the subconscious mind and allows the oxygen to circulate in the blood which reduces the amount of stress hormones in the body (remember, fear increases stress hormones in the bloodstream). Deep breathing also changes brain waves and brain patterns, making it easier to use your conscious mind to reprogram your subconscious mind.

Oftentimes, I advise my clients who are experiencing issues with fear to take up yoga or other meditative activity. Like everyone else, they tend to live in the past and in the future with little conscious attention paid to the present moment. For example, they focus on their past experiences with fear and project those experiences into what they fear might happen in the future. They focus on their automatic, habitual fear responses and have their foggy Fear eye glasses on. This impacts their ability to focus on their issue with fear in the present moment.

I find that yoga complements our sessions in that through their yoga practice, they learn about the importance of focusing on the present, being non-judgemental about their performance, breathing deeply, and maintaining a positive attitude. For example, research shows that people who are thinking negative or fearful thoughts have a particular pattern of activity in their prefrontal cortex compared to people who are thinking positive thoughts. After relaxation and meditation, the researchers found that people who had originally had negative or fearful thoughts had shifted the activity in their prefrontal cortex which then resembled the activity of the people with positive thoughts.

People who practice yoga or meditate learn to slow down or stop the "noise" in their brain and in their mind. As such, they're better able to experience the present moment, to be "in the moment" and see things clearly rather than being hindered by thoughts about the past or the future.

But you don't have to practice yoga to learn how to become mindful; anything that causes you to relax and calm your mind and body, stop focusing on negative emotions of the past, and direct your attention towards the present moment will allow your subconscious mind to focus on your positive, fearLESS goals. In order to increase you mindfulness, you need to:

1. *Focus on the moment.* Whenever you feel yourself experiencing fear, just focus on the moment. Don't let your mind wander to how you thought, felt or acted fearfully in the past or how this moment might be an indication of how you'll react in the future. If you indulge this wandering of the brain and subconscious mind, you'll end up triggering a stress response and reinforce your fear response.

2. *Be non-judgemental.* Don't judge yourself but rather just observe and accept yourself. Once you've made the observation let it go. Don't let a momentary thought, feeling or act of fear upset you; that moment has passed and judging it makes no difference to the present. Just let it inform you and use it to create positive, not negative energy.

3. *Remember to focus on one aspect of awareness at a time*. For example, you might want to first start with noticing how you breathe. Are you a shallow breather? Most of the time our fearful, mindless breathing is shallow and it's only when we focus our attention on our breathing that we can consciously make the effort to breathe more deeply and oxygenate our blood to release the stress hormones that have accumulated in our internal systems.

4. *Don't get upset if your mind wanders*. Achieving mindfulness takes practice. But like all things, the more you practice, the easier it will become.

How to Take a Fear Trigger Audit

In order to confront and overcome your fear response, you need to become sensitive to your emotional signals of fear, not just your physiological ones (e.g., racing heart, sweating palms, etc.). You need to develop an awareness of what your feelings represent. Feelings are like the proverbial canary in the coal mine; they tell us what's going on in our subconscious mind even if we're not consciously aware of why we're feeling the way we are. Remember, our feelings are a result of our thoughts, even our unconscious ones.

We can learn to manage our emotional fears when we find out what triggers them. When we learn the link between what we're feeling and what triggers those emotions, the more likely we'll be to determine whether our emotions are appropriate to the situation or not (e.g., whether a fear response is appropriate or not). One way to determine this "appropriateness' is to take an audit of what triggers our emotions.

Because much of what you experience occurs below your conscious awareness (remember, your subconscious mind takes in everything and stores it permanently), your subconscious mind may send fight-or-flight signals directly to your amygdala; bypassing your conscious mind and your prefrontal cortex. For example, you may find yourself going about your day-to-day business when you suddenly find yourself feeling anxious, nervous or fearful. Whenever that happens, your subconscious mind is trying to tell you something.

In order to understand what that something is, you need to determine if your fear reaction has been triggered by something or someone that you may not have consciously noticed.

To perform a fear trigger audit, you need to:

1. ***Do an environmental scan.*** Look around you. Focus on everything you see and try to determine if your fear has been triggered by that someone or something. For example, is someone in the room acting in a highly emotional state? Research has shown that emotion is contagious (remember, the consequences of indirect conditioning) and so your fear response may be a mirroring of someone else's fear.

2. ***Take your time and listen to your body.*** Don't just give each possibility a passing nod. Take the time, about 5 seconds, to seriously consider and feel the impact on your body as you think about what you're seeing as a possible trigger.

3. ***Develop your self-awareness.*** Remember, the more you can objectively explore your internal systems, the more you'll be able to recognize, identify and label your feelings. Use the audit whenever you have a fear response. You may notice certain patterns you have about what triggers you, how you're feeling and how you might be getting in your way of overcoming your fears. Remember, you're free to choose how you interpret things; you're free to choose how you think, feel and how you respond to a fear trigger.

Special Bonus Offers!

If you'd like more information about life transformation including: overcoming fear barriers; gaining confidence; overcoming emotional blocks and negative conditioning; and, eliminating other barriers to your personal and professional success, please visit the **www.wired2succeed.com** website where you will find several valuable gifts that include:

- a gift of **$500 in FREE online video and audio training**
- **FREE subscription to my** *Wired4Wisdom* electronic newsletter providing proven tips and strategies for a PowerFULL life
- **FREE membership in my** *PowerLines* daily inspiration club
- additional **FREE online "***Power Tools***"**
- **VIP invitation** to join hundreds of others who are motivated to overcome their fear barriers in my *Fearless and Fabulous!* **webinar coaching series**
- Plus, to reward you for taking the first step toward transforming your life by purchasing *Dump Your Fear!*, I'm offering you an *exclusive scholarship* to attend a *Power Charged LIVE!* **seminar**. As an additional bonus, you will be able to bring one guest to help them transform their lives too! That's a total value of $2994 which I'm reducing up to $2200 because I believe that you truly do want to succeed in life. This special offer is available to purchasers of *Dump Your Fear!* by Jacinth Tracey and is limited to one lifetime scholarship for two people per copy of *Dump Your Fear!* purchased.

Scholarship may only be applied to the Power Charged LIVE! seminar and registration is subject to availability and/or changes to program schedule. This scholarship may not be combined with any other promotions for the Power Charged LIVE! seminar. This is a strictly time-limited offer and the scholarship must be redeemed by the date shown on the **www.wired2succeed.com** website.

I'm committed to helping people — just like you — overcome any and all barriers getting in the way of their personal and professional success. My mission is to educate, inspire, motivate and transform the lives of anyone who is willing to finally stop living a "less than" life of default and step into their own personal power.

As I've shared with you throughout this book, I've also had to overcome significant fear barriers at many points in my life. I learned the hard way with my emotional and physical pain, as well as with my time, money and energy that fear will rob you of your life if you let it. Now I'm determined to help others — just like you — so that you don't have to go through what I did. It has become my life's mission to share my knowledge and experience and to shave off the 25-year learning curve so you will quickly and permanently transform your life into one filled with personal power, fearlessness and a real sense of purpose.

I am blessed to have books, seminars, webinars, workshops and speaking engagements that truly transform people's lives quickly and permanently. All those who've implement my holistic systems fully have gone on to overcome their past conditioning and have finally began to live happier and more fulfilled lives. Visit my **www.wired2succeed.com** website to see testimonials and hear from people who've gone on to success after having used my systems for life transformation.

I want you to transform your life as well. You deserve to live the life of your dreams. You deserve to overcome any and all obstacles getting in the way of your success. Just like I did and countless others who have implemented what I've taught them. So, from my heart to yours, I invite you to attend the next *Power Charged LIVE!* **seminar** and to join in the *Fearless and Fabulous!* **webinar series**. Each event will take you to an entirely new and higher level of success.

In the seminars and webinars, I'm able to drill down and elaborate on specific aspects of your mind, brain, body and spirit systems and rapidly increase your personal power. I take you step-by-step through the process of life transformation and show you the most efficient and proven methods to achieve lasting change. I reveal additional strategies that build on what you've learned in *Dump Your Fear!* to significantly increase your rate of transformation.

Whether it's overcoming fear barriers or other personal limitations, you will learn in my seminars and webinars exactly what it takes to become the person you've always wanted to be. To find out more and secure your spot, please register now at **www.wired2succeed.com** and change the course of your life forever.

Thank you for taking the time to read *Dump Your Fear!*. I wish you tremendous success in your life and look forward to meeting you online or in person soon.

To Your PowerFULL Life!

Jacinth Tracey

Your Top Ten Reasons to
CLAIM YOUR POWER NOW!

"When you use an excuse for not accomplishing something or not completing a project, you are actually giving power to someone or something outside of yourself."
Bob Proctor

10 Excuses to procrastinate	10 Reasons to Claim my Power Now!
1.	1.
2.	2.
3.	3.
4.	4.
5.	5.
6.	6.
7.	7.
8.	8.
9.	9.
10.	10.

PowerLines

*"Whatever we plant in our subconscious mind and nourish with
repetition and emotion will one day become a reality."*
Earl Nightingale

A power line is a cable that efficiently transfers large
quantities of electrical power from a power source to a demand
center. The PowerLines below will keep you connected to your
universal source of energy that feeds your internal systems;
particularly your subconscious mind (your demand center). Rip
out this page or write down these five motivational PowerLines
on a piece of paper. Put it in your wallet or your purse and take it
with you everywhere you go.

Whenever you find yourself battling with Fear, take a
moment to yourself and repeat these PowerLines at least 5 times
each. Focus, breathe and visualize yourself being in possession of
power and in control of your life. You'll see that the fear and
negative feelings fade away and that your sense of personal
power has increased.

My PowerLines

1. **I will do whatever I set my mind to**. My source of power is
   Universal Energy and that power is unlimited. As such, *my
   personal power is unlimited*.
2. *Today I will make the conscious choice to feel, think and act
   FearLESSly.*
3. *Today I will do one thing*—perform at least one action— *that puts
   me one step further toward the fulfillment of my goal* which is to
   overcome my fears.
4. *I am whatever I choose to become*. My past relationship with Fear
   is behind me and *my FearLESS future is certain*.
5. *I am already becoming the FearLESS and powerFULL person
   I've set out to become.*

JUST THE FACTS...

All the Fear Facts in *Dump Your Fear!* are listed here. They are written in the first-person — from your perspective — so that when you read or say them aloud, you will be incorporating what you read into the paradigms in your subconscious mind and increasing your level of self-awareness.

Read these as often as you can. Remember, repetition is how you help to rewire your brain and reprogram your subconscious mind to accept new thoughts, feelings and behaviors.

FEAR FACTS
1. Like all human beings, I have been born pre-wired for fear. It's a protective mechanism that keeps me from getting hurt.
2. When I feel fear it activates my body's fight-or-flight arousal system. It's an automatic reaction to feeling threatened.
3. Fear is just one of the ways that I can react emotionally to a stress trigger. I have a choice about how to react.
4. The way I respond to things, people and situations is based on my perception of whether or not they are stressors. I can change my perceptions any time I want to. It's within my control.
5. Most of my fears are learned and are not an inborn or natural part of who I am.
6. I learned (was conditioned) to fear certain things or situations from my own personal experience, especially during my childhood. I was not born with these fears.
7. I also learned (was conditioned) to fear certain things or situations by my early childhood conditioning, particularly by my family and other people in my social network.
8. The people and things in my environment, including the media, also conditioned me. They created fear and other negative emotions by influencing how I feel about myself.
9. Fear is a form of stress. It can either be acute (short-term) or chronic (long-term) in duration.

FEAR FACTS
10. I can develop physical health problems from being under chronic stress (such as habitually responding to stressors with fear).
11. I can develop mental health problems from being under chronic stress (such as habitually responding to stressors with fear).
12. When I habitually respond with fear to stressors, it's like I'm in a long-term relationship with a person named Fear. And just like I'm conditioned by my human relationships, I'm also being conditioned by Fear.
13. My internal and external systems work together to either reinforce my fears or help me to confront and overcome my fears.
14. My ongoing relationship with Fear affects my mental, physical and emotional systems.
15. Fear can cause me to think irrationally because the part of my brain responsible for logical thinking has been switched off when I'm experiencing a fear response.
16. Fear can cause me to temporarily forget familiar people and places, recent events, and even some of the personal details of my own life.
17. Fear lies to me by making me believe that the things I fear in my imagination are actually real.
18. Fear clouds my judgement and I can end up making foolish decisions that I later regret.
19. My fearful reaction to stressors is stored as permanent physical neurological changes in my brain.
20. The more often I've reacted to stressors with fear in the past, the easier it'll be for me to react with fear in the present and in the future.
21. Fear makes sure that my brain sends fight-or-flight messages to my body regardless of whether I'm reacting to a physical or emotional stressor.
22. Fear keeps me in fight-fight mode which makes me vulnerable to acute and chronic physical illnesses.
23. My mind is the ultimate control centre and guides everything I think, feel, say and do. All my fears originate in my mind. My brain is secondary to my mind.

FEAR FACTS
24. What I've told myself about what I fear and my ability to overcome my fear is deeply embedded not only in my brain, but more importantly, in my subconscious mind which always accepts the information I give it. It has no choice.
25. Over time my fearful response to stressors becomes automatic and mindless; bypassing my conscious mind, because I've wired my brain and subconscious mind for fear.
26. Fear makes me feel that there are limits to what I can do in my life. In reality, there are no limits. The only limits are those that I place on myself.
27. Living with fear is like I'm wearing a pair of foggy eye glasses. Because I can't see myself or my world clearly, I feel helpless to take any action.
28. Fear makes me feel that I can't do anything to change the situation I'm in or my life outcomes. In reality, I already have all the power I need to make any change I'd like.
29. Fear is a choice. It is a choice of where I choose to focus my attention and how I choose to interpret the things, situations and people in my environment.
30. Living in fear is a choice of orientation. Am I a fatalist (believing that things that happen to me are beyond my personal control) or an instrumentalist (believing that I can change my life by my own personal efforts and determination)?
31. My fearful thoughts lead to fearful feelings that lead to fearful actions. The end result is that my life outcomes are a reflection of my fearful thoughts, feelings and actions.
32. Personal power is all about being able to take control and responsibility for my thoughts, feelings and actions; to use my internal systems to drive me towards the achievement of my goals without violating the rights of others.
33. Increasing my self-awareness is important to overcoming my fears and is a necessary step before I can begin a lifelong relationship with Power.
34. My subconscious mind holds the key to re-programming and upgrading my internal operating systems; that is, my brain, mind and body.

FEAR FACTS
35. The results I get in life, my life outcomes, are a result of the actions set in motion by the workings of my conscious and subconscious mind.
36. When I set about to change my fear habit to a power habit, I'm adopting a new paradigm and changing lifelong conditioning. I need to be patient and not get discouraged by stops-and-starts in the process. I will succeed in over-riding my old dysfunctional paradigms and fear conditioning.
37. My subconscious mind is what connects me to my unlimited power source which is universal energy.
38. It takes a lot more energy to remain in my dysfunctional relationship with Fear than it does to confront him and move on to a healthy lifelong relationship with Power.
39. Fear is not only a negative emotion but it is also negative energy coursing through my internal systems. This negative energy is what is being sent out into the universe through my subconscious mind.
40. FearFULL thoughts (including the words I use in my self-talk) are also negative energy. Negative self-talk will cause all the gears in my internal systems to generate negative energy.
41. My life outcomes are the result of the type of energy I've attached to my thoughts, feelings and actions. The law of attraction allows me to attract positive things to myself if I make the conscious choice to think, feel and act fearLESSly.
42. I'm a spiritual being as well as an intellectual and emotional being. Using the power of spirit and universal energy is where I'll find my greatest power and reach my greatest potential.

On Silver Wings

I have a premonition that soars on silver wings.
It is a dream of your accomplishments
Of many wondrous things
I do not know beneath which sky
Or where you'll challenge fate.
I only know it will be high.
I only know it will be GREAT!

Anonymous.

It's Your Life …. Live it fearLESSly!

"Once a person is determined to help themselves, there is nothing that can stop them."
Nelson Mandela

Bibliography

The information contained in this book comes from a combination of the numerous books I've read over the course of a lifetime, the accumulated knowledge based on my university education and specialized training, and decades of personal and professional experience in mentoring and life transformation. The most valuable resources for *Dump Your Fear!* are listed below.

Anderson, Cameron, Keltner, Dacher and John, Oliver P. (2003). Emotional Convergence between People Over Time. *Journal of Personality and Social Psychology*, 84(5), 1054-1068.

Aronson, E. (2008). *The social animal* (10th Edition.). New York, NY, USA: Worth Publishers.

Ash, Mary Kay. (2003). *Miracles happen: The life and timeless principles of the founder of Mary Kay, Inc.* Quill, New York.

Bandura. Albert. (1982). Self-efficacy mechanism in human agency. *American Psychologist*, 37, 122-147.

Bandura, Albert. (1977). Self-efficacy: Toward a unifying theory of behavioral change, *Psychological Review*, 84, 191-215.

Bandura, Albert (1969). *Principles of Behavior Modification*. New York: Holt, Rhinehart and Winston, Inc.

Bechara, Antione, Damasio, Hanna and Damasio, Antonio. (2003). Role of the Amygdala in Decision-Making. *Annual New York Academy of Sciences*, 985, 356-369.

Bechara, Antoine. et al. (1999). Differential Contributions of the human amygdala and ventro-medial prefrontal cortex to decision-making. *Journal of Neuroscience,* 19, 5473-5481.

Bechara, Antoine. et al. (1994). Insensitivity to future consequences following damage to human prefrontal cortex. *Cognition,* 50, 7-15.

Best, Ben (2004). *The Amygdala and the Emotions.* www.benbest.com.

Bourne, Eugene (1995). *The Anxiety and Phobia Workbook.* Oakland, CA: New Harbinger Publications.

Bowman, Rachel et al. (2003 January). Stress Effects on Memory: Sex differences in performance. *Hormones and Behavior,* 43(1), 48–59.

Churchland, Patricia Smith (1986). *Neurophilosophy: Toward a Unified Science of the Mind-Brain.* USA, MIT Press.

Cohen S, Janicki-Deverts D, Miller GE (2007). Psychological stress and disease. *Journal of the American Medical Association,* 298(14), 1685–1687.

Cohen, S.; Kessler, R.C.; & Gordon, L.U. (1995). Strategies for measuring stress in studies of psychiatric and physical disorders. In Cohen, S.; Kessler, R.C.; & Gorden, L.U. (Eds.), *Measuring Stress. A Guide for Health and Social Scientists.* Oxford: Oxford University Press.

Colligan, Thomas, W. Colligan, MSW and Higgins M. (2006). Workplace Stress: Etiology and Consequences. *Journal of Workplace Behavioral Health,* 21(2), 89-97.

Cooper, Joel and Cooper, Grant (2002). Subliminal motivation: A story revisited. *Journal of Applied Social Psychology,* 32(11), 2213–2227.

Davis, M. (1992). The role of the amygdala in fear and anxiety. *Annual Review of Neuroscience,* 15, 353-375.

Davidson, R.J., & Sutton, S.K. (1995). *Affective neuroscience: The emergence of a discipline. Current Opinion in Neurobiology*, 5, 217-224.

DeSteno, D., R. E. Petty, D. T. Wegener, & D.D. Rucker (2000). Beyond valence in the perception of likelihood: The role of emotion specificity. *Journal of Personality and Social Psychology,* 78(3), 397–416.

Ekman, Paul (2003). *Emotions Revealed: Recognizing Faces and Feelings to Improve Communication.* New York: Henry Holt and Company.

Fiske, S. T. (2010). *Social beings: Core motives in social Psychology* (2nd Ed.). Hoboken, NJ: John Wiley & Sons, Inc.

Gabbard G.O. (2005) Mind, brain, and personality disorders. *American Journal of Psychiatry*, 162, 648-655.

Gleitman, Henry (1981). *Psychology.* New York: W.W.Norton & Company Inc.

Goleman, D. (1998). *Working with Emotional Intelligence.* New York: Bantam Books.

Gonzaga, Gian, C., Campos, Belinda, and Bradbury, Thomas (2007). Similarity, Convergence, and Relationship Satisfaction in Dating and Married Couples. *Journal of Personality and Social Psychology*, 93(1), 34-48.

Gray, J. A. (1987). *The Psychology of Fear and Stress* (2nd Edition). Cambridge: Cambridge University Press.

Gruber-Baldini, A.L., Shcaie, D.W., and Willis, S.L. (1995). Similarity in married couples: a longitudinal study of mental abilities and rigidity-flexibility. *Journal of Personality and Social Psychology*, 69, 191-203.

Hatfield, E., Cacioppo, J.T., and Rapson, R.L. (1994). *Emotional Contagion.* New York: Cambridge University Press.

Harvard Business Review. (2003 April). *Breakthrough Ideas for Tomorrow's Business Agenda.*

Hebb, Donald (1949). *The Organization of Behavior*. New York: Wiley.

Henry, O. & Evans, A.J. (2008). Occupational Stress in Organizations. *Journal of Management Research,* 8(3), 123–135.

Hill, Napoleon (2003). *Think and Grow Rich*. New York: Jeremy P. Tarcher/Penguin Group (USA) Inc.

Hiroto, D.S.; Seligman, M.E.P. (1975). Generality of learned helplessness in man. *Journal of Personality and Social Psychology,* 31, 311–327.

Jeffers, Susan (2007). *Feel the Fear...and do it Anyway*. New York: Ballantine Books.

Key, W.B. (1973) *Subliminal seduction: Ad media's manipulation of a not so innocent America.* Englewood Cliffs, NJ: Prentice-Hall.

Kivimäki, Mika (2012): Job strain as a risk factor for coronary heart disease: a collaborative meta-analysis of individual participant data. *The Lancet.* www.thelancet.com.

Knight, D.C. et al. (2004). Amygdala and hippocampal activity during acquisition and extinction of human fear conditioning. *Cognitive Affective and Behavioral Neuroscience,* 4, 317–325.

Kuchinke, Lars et al. (2005). Incidental effects of emotional valence in single word processing: an *f*MRI study. *NeuroImage,* 28, 1022-1032.

Kuhlmann, S., Piel, M., Wolf, O.T. (2005). Impaired Memory Retrieval after Psychosocial Stress in Healthy Young Men. *Journal of Neuroscience,* 25(11), 2977-2982.

Larson, Christian D. (1912). *Your Forces and How to Use Them.* Chicago: The New Literature Publishing Company.www.sacred-texts.com.

Lazarus, Richard S. (1966). *Psychological Stress and the Coping Process*. New York: McGraw-Hill.

Lazarus, Richard S. (1999). *Stress and Emotion: A New Synthesis*. New York: Springer Publishing.

Lee, Su Young et. al. (2011 February). Differential priming effect for subliminal fear and disgust facial expressions. *Attention, Perception, & Psychophysics*, 2(73), 473–481.

Levi, Lennart (1971). *Society, Stress and Disease*. New York: Oxford University Press.

Levenson RW, and Ruef AM. (1992). Empathy: a physiological substrate. *Journal of Personality and Social Psychology*, 63, 234–246.

Lieberman, M.D. (2007). Social Cognitive Neuroscience: A Review of Core Processes. *Annual Review of Psychology,* 58, 259–289.

Makeig S, Gramann K, Jung T, Sejnowski T J, and Poizner H. (2009 August). Linking brain, mind and behavior. *International Journal of Psychophysiology*, 73(2), 95-100.

McClellan, Stephanie and Hamilton, Beth. 2010. *So Stressed: The Ultimate Stress-Relief Plan for Women*. New York: Free Press.

McConnell, James V. (1977). *Understanding Human Behavior* (2nd Edition). New York. Holt, Rinehart and Winston.

Mirowsky, John and Ross, Catherine (1986). Social Patterns of Distress. *Annual Review of Sociology,* 12, 23-45.

Mulryan, Chris (2011). *Acute Illness Management*. Thousand Oaks, California. Sage Publications Limited.

Murphy, Joseph (2008) *The Power of Your Sub-Conscious Mind*. Arthur Pell (Ed.) New York: Penguin Group.

Murphy, S.T. and Zajon, R.B. (1993). Affect, cognition and awareness: affective priming with optimal and suboptimal stimulus exposures. *Journal of Personality and Social Psychology*, 64(5), 723-739.

Myers, D. G. (2010). *Psychology* (9th Edition). New York: Worth Publishers.

Nauert, Rick (2007). *How Fear is Learned*. Psych Central. www.psychcentral.com.

Novaco, R. W. (2000). Anger. In A. E. Kazdin (Ed.), *Encyclopedia of psychology*. Washington, D.C.: American Psychological Association and Oxford University Press.

Novaco, R.W. (1986). Anger as a clinical and social problem. In R. Blanchard and C. Blanchard (Eds.), *Advances in the study of aggression*. Vol. II. New York: Academic Press.

Olsson, Andreas; Nearing, Katherine, I.; Phelps, Elizabeth. A. (March 2007). Learning fears by observing others: The neural systems of social fear transmission. *Social Cognitive and Affective Neuroscience*, 2(1), 3-11.

Olsson, Andreas and Phelps, Elizabeth, A. (2007). Social Learning of Fear. *Nature Neuroscience* 10(9), 1095-1102.

Pearlin, Leonard. Stress and Mental Health: A Conceptual Overview (1999). In Horwitz, Allan V. and Scheid, Teresa L.A (Eds.) *Handbook for the Study of Mental Health: Social Contexts, Theories and Systems*. Cambridge: Cambridge University Press, Pages 161-175.

Pearlin, Leonard et. al. (1981). The Stress Process. *Journal of Health and Social Behavior*, 22, 37-56.

Pearlin, Leonard and Lieberman, M.A. (1979). Social Sources of Emotional Stress. In R. Simmons (Ed.) *Research in Community and Mental Health*. Greenwich, CT: JAI, Pages.217-48

Peterson, C. (2003). Personal Control and Well-Being. In D. Kahneman, E. Diener, and N. Schwarz (Eds) *Well-being: The Foundations of Hedonic Psychology*. New York: Russell Sage Foundation, Pages 288–301.

Prochaska, J.O and Velicer, W.F. (Sep–Oct 1997). The transtheoretical model of health behavior change. *American Journal of Health Promotion*, 12(1), 38–48.

Proctor, Bob (2006). *Success Puzzle*. Audiobook and CD. LifeSuccess Publications. Scottsdale, Arizona.

Putnam, Hilary (1967). Psychological Predicates. In W. H. Capitan and D. D. Merrill (Eds.) *Art, Mind and Religion*. Pittsburgh: University of Pittsburgh Press.

University of California Irvine (2006 February). *Researchers Prove A Single Memory Is Processed In Three Separate Parts Of The Brain*. www.sciencedaily.com.

Roozendaal Benno, McEwen, Bruce S. and Chattarji, Sumantra (2009 June). Stress, memory and the amygdala. *Nature Reviews Neuroscience,* 10, 423–433.

Roth, S. (1980). A revised model of learned helplessness in humans. *Journal of Personality,* 48, 103–133.

Rotter, Julian (1966). Generalized Expectancies for Internal vs. External Control of Reinforcement. *Psychological Monographs,* 80, 1-28.

Sandi, Carmen and Pinelo-Nava, M. Teresa (2007 January). Stress and Memory: Behavioral Effects and Neurobiological Mechanisms. *Neural Plasticity,* 1–20.

Sapolsky R. M. (1996). Why stress is bad for your brain. *Science,* 273, 749-750.

Shreeve, James. Beyond the Brain. *National Geographic.* www.nationalgeographic.com

Seligman, M. E. P. (1972). Learned helplessness. *Annual Review of Medicine*, 23(1), 407-412.

Siegel, Daniel, J. (2011). *Mindsight: The New Science of Personal Transformation*. New York: Bantam Books Trade Paperbacks.

Sivanada, Swami Sri. 1997. *Thought Power (6ᵗʰ Edition)*. India: Divine Life Society Publication.

Smith, Edward and Kosslyn, Stephen (2007. *Cognitive Psychology: Mind and Brain*. New Jersey: Prentice Hall.

Stark, Rudolf et. al. (2006). Influence of the stress hormone cortisol on fear conditioning in humans: Evidence for sex differences in the response of the prefrontal cortex. *NeuroImage*, 32, 1290–1298.

Thompson, Curt (2010). *Anatomy of the Soul: Surprising connections between neuroscience and spiritual practices that can transform your life and relationships*. USA: Tyndale House Publishers Inc.

Ullman, Leonard P. and Krasner, Leonard (1969). *A Psychological Approach to Abnormal Behavior*. Englewood Cliffs, New Jersey. Prentice-Hall, Inc.

Vriends, N., et. al. (2011). The influence of state anxiety on the acquisition and extinction of fear. *Journal of Behavioural Therapy and Experimental Psychiatry*, 42, 46-53.

Wattles, Wallace D. (2010). *The Science of Getting Rich: The Original Classic.* United Kingdom: Capstone Publishing Ltd.

Wheaton, Blair (1999). The Nature of Stressors. In Horwitz, Allan V. and Scheid, Teresa L.A (Eds.) *Handbook for the Study of Mental Health: Social Contexts, Theories and Systems*. Cambridge: Cambridge University Press, Pages176-197.

Zinbarg, R. E. and Mohlman, J. (1998). Individual differences in the acquisition of affectivity valenced associations. *Journal of Personality and Social Psychiatry*, 74, 1024-1040.

Acknowledgements

It's customary for me to begin many of my seminars, conferences and webinars by asking my audience if they're familiar with the saying "The teacher will come when the student is ready." That's because I truly believe that teachers exist all around us in the form of experiences and specific people that teach us valuable lessons that help us to improve our lives.

Most of the time however, we're totally oblivious to these potentially life-changing lessons. We have foggy eye glasses on — based on our conditioning and subconscious paradigms— and don't see teaching moments even when they're right in front of us. It's only when we're aware and conscious of the fact that we need to widen our perspective and take in new information that we allow teachers to help us make the necessary mental, emotional and spiritual shifts that are necessary for our success.

I've been fortunate to have had many great teachers in my life. The first and foremost are my mother Yvonne and my maternal grandmother Mary. Together they taught me the value of a spiritual connection with a higher power — that there's someone greater than ourselves on whom we can rely for strength as we journey through life. The other teachers are my step-father (my dad) Calvin, my sister Paula, and my close friends and family who've helped me to grow and blossom into the person I am today.

More recently I've had the pleasure of meeting three new teachers. There's Noel Walrond who introduced me to Bob Proctor and the phrase "intuition is divine instruction" which has become a guiding philosophy in my life. There's Paul Bresge, my yoga teacher, in whose classes I learned to breathe deeply and quiet my internal systems long enough to feel the power of my own energy. In his classes I learned to become mindful and connect with my universal power source. And, then there's my most beloved teacher of all and my soul mate; my husband Joee. He's the man I always dreamed of marrying but never managed to find until I suspended my fearful disbelief of getting my "happily ever after". His love and support and unfailing enthusiasm at even my smallest accomplishments have taught me that the universe really does give you what you ask for and truly believe.

And thanks also to the hundreds of students, clients, employees, friends and even strangers that I've had the privilege of working with over the years. You've been great teachers. My work with you has given me a sense of joy, and also had the additional benefit of allowing me to test my theories in real-life and to experience additional epiphanies and "Aha!" moments. By helping you to overcome your fear barriers and embrace your personal power, I've been able to live out my worthy ideal. It's my sincere wish that everyone comes to realize that living a life of fear and "what if's" denies the true power that lies within all of us, and that our innate power is ready to lead us to success, if we'll just get out of our own way.

About the Author

Jacinth Tracey is a life transformation and mindset mentor, author and internationally-recognized speaker. For over 25 years, she's been known for her academic publications and expertise in mental and physical health. She founded **Wired2Succeed** to help people — just like you — to overcome barriers to their success, reclaim their personal power, and take control of their lives.

She's rapidly gained a following for her approach to life transformation. Her holistic approach incorporates principles from such fields as mental health, biology, psychology, neuroscience, and spirituality. This holistic approach places particular emphasis on a mind-brain-body-spirit connection. This proven system, combined with her use of relatable real-life examples, ultimately leads to "Aha!" moments and profound shifts in people's thoughts, feelings and actions. Used in combination with the proven tools that she provides to help eliminate lifelong negative thought and behavior patterns, her clients forever change their understanding of what it takes to overcome their fears and get the successful life of their dreams.

Jacinth is happily married to her soul mate and the man of her dreams, Joee. Their story is a true reminder that the universe will conspire to give us everything we want, once we make the conscious decision that we want it. Jacinth's life is a living testament to the success of her life transformation systems and the fact that it's never too late to begin to go after and start living life by our own design, rather than living our life by default.

Please visit **www.wired2succeed.com** for more information or email any enquiries to **info@wired2succeed.com** and to **book Jacinth for your next speaking engagement.**

www.ingramcontent.com/pod-product-compliance
Lightning Source LLC
Chambersburg PA
CBHW020658270326
41928CB00005B/177